FIT TO FLY
A MEDICAL HANDBOOK FOR PILOTS

FIT TO FLY
A MEDICAL HANDBOOK FOR PILOTS
Second Edition

Compiled by The Medical Study Group
British Air Line Pilots Association

BSP PROFESSIONAL BOOKS

OXFORD LONDON EDINBURGH

BOSTON PALO ALTO MELBOURNE

Copyright © by British Air Line Pilots'
    Association 1980, 1988

All rights reserved. No part of this
publication may be reproduced, stored
in a retrieval system, or transmitted,
in any form or by any means, electronic,
mechanical, photocopying, recording
or otherwise without the prior
permission of the copyright owner.

First published in Great Britain by
    Granada Publishing Limited
    – Technical Books Division, 1980
Second edition published by
    BSP Professional Books, 1988

British Library
Cataloguing in Publication Data

British Air Line Pilots' Association
    Medical Study Group
    Fit to fly.—2nd ed.
    1. Commercial aircraft. Pilots. Physical
    fitness – Manuals
    I. Title
    613.7

ISBN 0–632–02398–8

BSP Professional Books
A division of Blackwell Scientific
    Publications Ltd
Editorial Offices:
Osney Mead, Oxford OX2 0EL
    (Orders: Tel. 0865 240201)
8 John Street, London WC1N 2ES
23 Ainslie Place, Edinburgh EH3 6AJ
3 Cambridge Center, Suite 208,
    Cambridge, MA 02142, USA
667 Lytton Avenue, Palo Alto, California
    94301, USA
107 Barry Street, Carlton, Victoria 3053,
    Australia

Printed and bound in Great Britain by
    Guernsey Press

Contents

Acknowledgements

The Medical Study Group of the British Airline Pilots' Association is very grateful for the help, criticism and encouragement given by many medical experts who are in no way connected with the Association and whose advice was freely given. In particular, the Association wishes to thank:

British Airways Medical Services.
Medical Department – Civil Aviation Authority, UK.
Ross Institute of Hygiene and Tropical Medicine, London.
RAF Institute of Aviation Medicine, Farnborough.
British Caledonian Airways Medical Department.
Royal College of Physicians, London.

In addition the Study Group also wishes to freely acknowledge the following authors and publishers for their kind permission to use illustrations, background material, extracts, or to quote from:

Physiology of Flight: Dr C. R. Harper and Dr G. J. Kidera – published by United Airlines, USA.
Facts about Alcohol, illustration from an advisory leaflet – published by the Health Education Council, London.
Black's Medical Dictionary – published by Adam and Charles Black, London.
Encyclopaedia Britannica – published by Encyclopaedia Britannica International Ltd, London and USA.
Medical Handbook for Pilots –published by Department of Transportation, Federal Aviation Administration, USA.
Aeromedicine for Aviators: Dr K. E. E. Read – published by Pitman Publishing Ltd, London.
New Essential First Aid and *New Safety and First Aid*: Ward Gardner and Roylance – published by Pan Books Ltd, London.

The Illustrated Family Medical Encyclopaedia (some of the text from chapter 7: Tropical Hygiene) – published by The Reader's Digest Association Ltd, London.

The three paragraphs in inverted commas on pages 44 and 45 are quoted from Dr Malcolm Jayson's article 'Backache: A Matter of Structural Distress' which appeared in the *New Scientist*, 12th August 1976.

Illustrations at the beginning of each chapter were specially commissioned and executed by Martin Eaglen, Lewes, Sussex, who regularly contributes to the Association's house journal, *The Log*.

Introduction

By Doctor M. F. P. Marshall *Association Medical Adviser*

Pilots have become increasingly aware of the importance of taking positive action to try to maintain a high standard of health. By so doing, not only do they improve their chances of keeping their licences until retirement, but they also find that they can operate more efficiently and are better able to cope with the discomforts and stresses of their profession.

This revised edition of the medical handbook has been produced as an aid for pilots; it has been written by pilots and is presented in a style and language which should, hopefully, be easy to ready and understand.

The medical facts have, as far as possible, been verified as accurate. However, where there is some divergence of opinion amongst medical experts one line has to be taken, even though this will inevitably lead to some disagreement between the medical authorities.

In a handbook of this type some overlap of subject matter is unavoidable in different chapters, but these instances are valuable in illustrating the interdependence of the various subjects. Each chapter has been discussed in detail by The Medical Study Group, and it says much for the tolerance of the individual contributors that they have accepted so much criticism and in some cases have allowed drastic cuts and changes to be made.

The contents of the handbook have been divided into nine chapters. The first of these covers the very pertinent subject of physical fitness. The next chapter deals with the many aspects of mental fitness, concentrating particularly on stress. Advice is also given on alcoholism and controversial subjects such as biorhythms are discussed. Following the simple advice given in the chapter on diet can make an important contribution to the health of the pilot, and to air safety in general. Guidance is then given in dealing with the problems of sleep and on the effects of interference with the body's circadian rhythms. In this chapter

(4), Section F, Soporifics, in the section devoted to pre-flight sleep, has been re-written and expanded, in the light of more recent knowledge.

In the two sections on aviation physiology (chapters 5 and 6), it was important to include the essentials, but the range of the subject matter is so large that inevitably much has had to be omitted. It is thought that the information given is not only adequate for a handbook of this nature, but may perhaps stimulate further reading.

Chapter 6 includes some of the more common diseases and conditions which are of particular concern to aircrew, such as coronary heart disease. Again, a few thoughts on 'passive smoking', to supplement Section C, Cigarette smoking, under the first section on heart disease, have been added at the end of this chapter. Aviation aspects of defects of ocular and auditory function are also considered, and advice on the prevention of backache is given. In Chapter 7, on tropical medicine, advice was sought directly from the Ross Institute of Hygiene and Tropical Medicine. There is also a chapter (8) on first aid which has been included in the handbook for completeness. There are first aid chapters in various flight manuals, but the basic common-sense advice given here is readily available for reference. The legal implications are also briefly discussed.

Chapter 9, new to this second edition, has been added to provide a brief insight into a topic which has attracted growing interest in recent years – aviation psychology, or human factors. In the automated flight decks of new generation aircraft, often with a reduced crew comple-ment, a better understanding of man's interface with his operating environment and of his relationship with his fellow crew members is of importance.

Finally, an additional Appendix (2), has been included to provide some general information on a topic of international public concern, AIDS, together with appropriate 'helpline' telephone numbers. This essentially summarises the more extensive briefings provided to those in the aviation industry and to the public at large.

It is hoped that this handbook, which has been produced by the hard work of their colleagues, will prove to be of value to pilots, not only as a reference book, but also to give a stimulus to other aircrew who wish to improve their understanding of the medical problems of their profession.

1 Physical Fitness and Flying

An airline pilot is a member of a medically select group, starting his career free from medical abnormalities, and in good physical condition. However, with the advent of modern, highly automated, power-controlled transport aircraft, the necessity for aircrew to maintain this high standard of physical fitness is perhaps not as evident as it was in the past. Apart from the obvious fact that more than minimal amounts of strength, co-ordination, endurance and alertness are required at the start of duty in order to ensure an adequate performance for the last landing of the day, why should we bother ourselves with physical fitness?

11

Consider these facts:

(a) Physical fitness enables toleration of greater physical stress, and reduces the effects of fatigue.

(b) It gives one a sense of well-being, with the accompanying feeling of greater mental alertness. Physical exercise assists in relieving the nervous tensions and stresses of the day.

(c) Regular exercise burns up those excess calories, reduces body fat, and even tends to cut down cholesterol levels in the blood.

(d) Fitness improves heart muscle circulation, and helps to reduce blood pressure.

(e) Finally, and probably most importantly, it can play a part in avoiding heart disease. Together with smoking and obesity, inactivity is one of the prime contributors to coronary heart disease. Flying a transport aircraft is an especially sedentary occupation interspersed with sudden short periods of high mental workload and stress. These can trigger off the body's alarm system which releases extra fat and sugar into the blood in preparation for intense physical activity. Ironically, this activity does not follow in routine airline flying; instead, the extra fat and sugar can contribute to the furring-up of our coronary vessels. So the pilot who is physically fit and takes regular exercise will be far better placed in combating these dangers than his overweight and slothful colleague.

An impressive list indeed; more so when you consider that it is *not* necessary to be a super athlete to obtain these benefits. *It is sufficient that exercise is taken regularly, frequently, and that it raises the pulse-rate so that you feel you have extended yourself.* Therefore, even digging the garden, or going for a brisk uphill walk, if done for, say, a quarter of an hour, three times a week, will straightaway be beneficial.

However, since the ultimate aim is to provide an overall fitness in the cardiovascular, respiratory and muscular areas, it follows that the most beneficial types of exercise are those that involve plenty of movement and which get the heart and lungs working well. Most active sports are ideal; running, swimming, cycling, tennis, squash etc. However, 'body-building' type exercises, weight-lifting, and suchlike are not recommended, since they do not stimulate the heart and lungs to the same extent.

A few words of caution

(a) If you have spent the last twenty years getting out of shape, do not expect to become fit over-night. There is a preliminary period during which anybody not used to regular activity must become conditioned to moderate exercise, before any strenuous activity is undertaken. The older the individual, the longer this period of preparation should be. Start getting fit **slowly**, and progress at a steady, but slow rate, as the capacity for effort without distress increases. At all costs avoid a pattern of long periods of inactivity interspersed with sudden bursts of strenuous exercise. Remember, exercise regularly, frequently and *within* your capabilities.

(b) Do not start vigorous exercise following a heavy meal. Wait at least two hours, because digestive processes within the body tend to divert blood from the heart and brain during the period following eating.

(c) Warm up adequately before any work-out. (Stretching exercises such as arm-circling and toe-touching are fine for this purpose.)

(d) Do not over-exert yourself and allow a cooling-off period at the end of your activity. Five minutes spent tapering off gradually will help avoid any nausea or muscle cramps. Finally, in the unlikely event of exercise precipitating any serious discomfort, some suggested remedial action is listed at the end of this chapter.

Since each person is at a different level of physical fitness, there can be no one series of activities that will maintain a satisfactory level for everyone. Those who wish to obtain the fullest benefits will require a tailored fitness programme that first evaluates the individual and then the sports facilities available.

Whilst there are many books on the subject of exercise programmes for the enthusiast, circuit training can be recommended as providing a maximum of flexibility with a minimum of equipment. Basically one sets out a number of 'stations' (usually five) in a circuit, 20–25 feet apart. Each 'station' consists of an exercise that is specific to a given part of the body (e.g. press-ups for arms and shoulders, sit-ups for abdomen etc). The training consists of running from one 'station' to the next and performing a set number of the given exercises at each. By varying the type and number of exercises, the speed of running and the overall time spent, any desired level of fitness can be reached and maintained. In limited space, the 'stations' can all be in one place, with the distance apart simulated by running three or four laps of the room. In the confines of a hotel room, it would probably best be accomplished by running on the spot.

Exercising while on duty is, to say the least, impractical; however, when flying *do* get out of your seat and walk around at least every hour. This improves and increases the circulation of the blood, alleviates backache and muscle cramps and generally helps in clearing the head and fighting fatigue, especially on long night sectors.

Backache itself is a problem common to pilots and exercise is very useful in the avoidance of back disorders and the maintenance of good postural muscles and mobility of joints in the spine. For those suffering from the odd twinges, a set of exercises specifically designed to strengthen the back muscles can be found in the Appendix on page 76.

Modern technology constantly tempts us into leading a life of ease, inactivity and passive participation. **Don't.** Activity and vigorous expression are two of the body's basic needs; hence attaining and maintaining physical fitness will be contributing to a fuller and more active life.

Warning signals and what to do about them

This is *not* meant to deter anyone from getting fit! However, there is a chance that exercising may trigger off a latent disorder; hence the advice offered here:

(a) Should you feel any abnormalities in heart rate and pulse, pain or pressure in the centre of the chest, arm or throat, during or following exercise; *stop* the exercise and see your doctor – there is a possibility of a heart problem.

(b) Any feelings of dizziness, lightheadedness, cold sweat or fainting; stop the exercise and lie down with the feet elevated or put your head down between the legs until the symptoms pass. These symptoms are caused by an insufficient blood flow to the brain, and you should see your doctor before undertaking any further exercise.

(c) If there is a persistent rapid heart rate 5–10 minutes after stopping exercise, the exercise was probably too vigorous. Next time take it easier, and increase the vigour of exercise more slowly. See your doctor if the recovery rate still remains excessively high.

(d) If there is any flare-up of arthritic conditions or pain and soreness in joints during or after exercise; *rest*, and do not resume the exercise programme until the condition has subsided, then exercise at a lower level.

(e) Prolonged fatigue after exercise indicates too vigorous activity. Nausea or vomiting after exercise also indicates exercising too vigorously or cooling off too quickly.

2 Mental Fitness

It has been said in the past that a mentally-unstable pilot is more danger to the operation than one with a 'dicky' heart. Certainly in these days of incapacitation-trained crews, a physically sick pilot can be coped with safely and efficiently. However, this cannot be said for the pilot with psychological problems. Even if the mental disorder were obvious to the other members of his crew, he might well strongly resent any suggestion that he be relieved of his duties, and thus present even more of a danger. Mental fitness is, therefore, of vital importance, and may be conveniently considered under a series of sub-headings.

Stress

Stress is not in itself harmful – indeed a certain amount of it is desirable. Only the extremes cause problems. Little or no stress results in under-

16

stimulation. Excessive stress is more common, but this should be amenable to diagnosis – both in oneself and one's colleagues.

Attempts have been made to quantify temporary stress to various situations, the theory being that all change is to some extent stressful. The snag with this theory is that individual tolerance to stress varies so widely. Although allocating precise figures may be impossible, it should be recognised that all of us show some reaction to stress, and that if this stress becomes intolerable our mental health and job performance will suffer.

Because stress is a permanent feature of modern life, a very low stress tolerance is obviously undesirable in a pilot. Unfortunately, with certain individuals, their ability to cope deteriorates with age. A low stress tolerance may manifest itself by excessive smoking or drinking, extreme nervousness, or other behavioural abnormalities; clearly there may come a time when such people become a hazard to themselves and the general public, in which case treatment or premature retirement must be considered.

Forms of relaxation like meditation or yoga are favoured by some as an antidote to stress, but for most of us a recognition that the problem exists should be sufficient. Be aware that all of us, even you, can suffer from stress symptoms under the wrong combination of circumstances. An immediate antidote may well be found by taking a holiday, or devoting extra time to relaxation, an outside interest, or a hobby. When stress becomes extreme, consideration should be given to taking some time off or seeking advice until the problem is resolved; overstress should not be confused with character defects or malingering.

Body rhythms

Human health and behaviour fluctuates in a complex pattern of short- and long-term rhythms. Their periodicity varies from a few hours in some body processes, up to many days for complex functions (such as the menstrual cycle in women). Most of us recognise in ourselves when we have mental and physical 'good' and 'bad' days. Ideally, further recognition of this factor should be reflected by a greater flexibility in our work patterns. Attempts to quantify the long term rhythms have spawned the minor industry known as 'biorhythms', which sells slide-rules for calculating one's good and bad periods. It bases its calculations on date of birth. Some public transport companies in Japan and Switzerland have claimed a greatly reduced accident rate by rostering employees in accordance with their biorhythmic patterns; however, most authorities regard biorhythms as being little better than astrology. A practical and reliable method of allowing for the fluctuations in human performance has yet to be developed.

Fatigue

Fatigue and sleep disruption are potent factors in lowering one's mental fitness. Extreme sleep deprivation may lead to irrational behaviour, with latent eccentricities coming to the surface, and a marked deterioration in job performance and decision-making; it may even precipitate an attack of epilepsy in people with no previous history of the disease. By definition, an exhausted pilot cannot be mentally fully fit.

Alcoholism

Alcoholism is *not* a failure of one's moral fibre or stiff upper lip; it is a disease. The transition from heavy drinking to alcoholism is ill-defined, so what begins as an occasional release from reality may eventually become a habit. Alcohol can lower an individual's tolerance to stress, thus aggravating an original problem. Some doctors now suggest that a predisposition towards alcoholism may in fact be indicated by certain slight abnormalities in a person's body chemistry. Alcohol is a depressant. Its effect on physical and mental behaviour is represented in the illustration opposite.

The 'danger signs' of alcoholism are as follows:

(a) Surreptitious drinking.

(b) A few 'quickies' prior to meeting people.

(c) Becoming regularly intoxicated.

(d) Increasingly large amounts of alcohol required to get drunk.

(e) Drinking alone.

(f) Drinking for its own sake, rather than socially.

US Federal Aviation Regulations define alcoholism as 'a condition in which a person's intake of alcohol is great enough to damage his physical

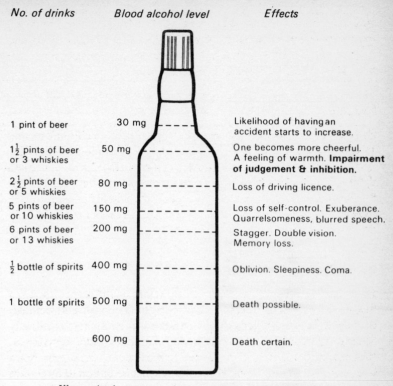

No. of drinks	Blood alcohol level	Effects
1 pint of beer	30 mg	Likelihood of having an accident starts to increase.
1½ pints of beer or 3 whiskies	50 mg	One becomes more cheerful. A feeling of warmth. **Impairment of judgement & inhibition.**
2½ pints of beer or 5 whiskies	80 mg	Loss of driving licence.
5 pints of beer or 10 whiskies	150 mg	Loss of self-control. Exuberance. Quarrelsomeness, blurred speech.
6 pints of beer or 13 whiskies	200 mg	Stagger. Double vision. Memory loss.
½ bottle of spirits	400 mg	Oblivion. Sleepiness. Coma.
1 bottle of spirits	500 mg	Death possible.
	600 mg	Death certain.

Illustration by courtesy of The Health Education Council

health or personal or social functioning'. As with all diseases, early diagnosis is essential if therapy is to stand a reasonable chance of success. One American airline, famous for its anti-alcoholism efforts, claims an 80% recovery rate in motivated patients; this sort of success rate declines rapidly if a 'head in the sand' attitude is adopted, or the symptoms are not spotted at an early stage. Unfortunately, alcoholism is all too often not diagnosed until the disease is well advanced. This is partly because it is still something of a taboo sickness, which people prefer to pretend does not exist, and partly because it is a great mimic of other diseases. As a result the seriousness of alcoholism is masked. It can only be beaten by a three-pronged attack from pilots, management and pilot association; it is an issue which should not be shirked.

Finally, bear in mind that the ruling advocating abstinence from alcohol within eight hours prior to duty is only a protection against *moderate* amounts of alcohol. Efficiency is noticeably reduced when suffering from a hangover. In fact, the liver takes three hours to eliminate the alcohol contained in one pint of beer.

Drugs

If you are ill enough to require medication, you should not be flying (with the qualification that there are a few drugs which may safely be taken, *under the strict supervision of an aviation doctor*).

If you are likely to be flying in the near future, be very cautious in the use of sleeping tablets, antibiotics, sulpha drugs, 'pep' pills, sedatives and antihistamines (present in many 'cold cures', anti-allergy preparations, nose-drops and sprays). We are all fully aware of the effects of alcohol, but remember that even small amounts of alcohol greatly magnify the effects of other drugs. Finally on this subject, do not forget that, following any local or general, dental or other anaesthetics, you should not fly for at least twenty-four hours.

Mental illness

According to Civil Aviation Authority statistics, mental illness is second only to cardiovascular disease in the premature career termination league. These CAA figures are probably an under-statement because many cases of mental illness undoubtedly escape into other statistical pigeon-holes such as early retirement, failed competency checks or apparent physical causes. Because the brain is by far the most complex organ of the human body, diagnosing mental illness in its early stages is particularly difficult. For pilots the important thing to remember is that mental illness is comparatively common, difficult to spot, and requires the understanding and concern of everyone. Therefore, whenever mental illness is suspected, the only sensible course of action is referral to an expert for diagnosis and eventual treatment.

Counselling services

Some pilot associations have found peer group counselling services to be of value. Pilot counsellors will not normally provide their own expertise, but in the first place only lend a sympathetic ear to a colleague and 'share a burden'. Counsellors will, however, have a full range of expert services available and the ultimate aim must be to try and persuade 'patients' to make use of these services. Any such scheme must be based on the word TRUST, with all counsellors committed to absolute confidentiality.

3 Diet Guidance

This guide is not for fanatics. Teetotal, non-smoking vegetarians, who climb mountains before breakfast, clearly need no advice, while anyone dedicated only to the abuse of his body needs little more than the name of a good funeral director. The following suggestions are offered in the belief that most of us fall somewhere between these extremes; our aim is an enjoyable life, but also a healthy and reasonably long one. Dietary experts may fall out over details, but most of them would agree that the food we eat profoundly affects our health and longevity.

Amount of food

Although individual needs naturally vary, there is little doubt that most people in the affluent world eat too much. In parts of the Caucasus and

Andes, centenarians are commonplace and senior citizens touching 120 years old not unusual; investigations into the reason for such longevity have discovered that these people differ from western man in that they eat very little food – sometimes almost a malnutrition level. Although other factors, such as heredity and exercise may well play a part, there is much evidence to suggest that gluttony is indeed a 'deadly' sin.

Type of food

Based on what is good for your 'plumbing' rather than your palate, we can compile a rough and ready 'Bad Food Guide'.

(a) Aim for a well balanced diet; cut down particularly on *sugar* and *fats*.

(b) In cooking, avoid frying foods; concentrate more on boiling, stewing or grilling.

(c) Poultry and fish are preferable to fatty red meats and offal.

(d) Keep most dairy produce and eggs to a minimum – they are high in cholesterol.

(e) Provide roughage with fresh vegetables and fruit, or better still bran – this will help to maintain healthy bowels.

(f) Eat little and often, rather than very heavy meals taken infrequently. The stomach empties in two and one half hours – if the interval is too prolonged the excess acids can give trouble.

(g) Avoid adding excessive amounts of salt as this can elevate the blood pressure.

In some instances the link between diet and disease is as yet rather tenuous; for example, some doctors – but by no means all – believe that cancers, multiple sclerosis, arthritis and diabetes, can be caused, controlled or modified by diet. More generally accepted is the link between coronary heart disease (CHD) and excessive fat intake. CHD, now the number one killer in the western world, is fast reaching epidemic proportions; it is also largely 'self-inflicted', because CHD could be almost eliminated – at least for persons in the prime of life – by two simple rules: stop smoking and eat less fat.

Fat is, therefore, the number one villain in our 'Bad Food Guide'. Word has got around that vegetable fats are rather less lethal than animal fats, but in fact a large body of medical evidence rejects this 'margarine myth', and suggests that the intake of *all* fats should be reduced. The problem is that if too much fat is consumed, it tends to infiltrate the blood stream and sludge up the arteries. The effect is twofold:

Fatty sludge may block a blood vessel. When this happens in the heart, the result is a 'heart attack' – an increasingly common form of sudden death. When it occurs in the brain, the result is a 'stroke', often manifested by partial paralysis.

Less dramatic is the more chronic result of polluted arteries known as tissue anoxia. The function of blood is to transport oxygen to the most far-flung outposts of the human body; in spite of what the Bible may say, 'the staff of life' is not bread, but oxygen, without which we rapidly expire. Fat sludge on the walls of the blood capillaries hinders this transfer of oxygen, leaving the poor old body permanently gasping and below par. Tissue anoxia has been mentioned as a possible cause of cancers and senility – it certainly cannot do you much good.

Now some statistics to put the ogre of 'fat' into perspective:

(a) In the affluent (CHD-prone) world, fat typically comprises about 40% of calories consumed.

(b) In those countries where CHD is rare, fat intake is normally less than 20% of calories consumed.

(c) It has been proved that one can thrive on a diet containing less than 1% fat!

The answer is obviously to reduce our fat intake to more sensible proportions, but there are two main barriers to this: habit and convenience.

Habit: if we have breakfasted on fried eggs and bacon every day for the last thirty years, this diet's chief attraction is probably its familiarity. So make an effort, try a change. Other breakfasts are just as – or even more – palatable.

Convenience: probably the simplest way to mass-produce food is to throw a piece of meat or fish into a pan of fat, but your arteries would appreciate it if you sometimes sought out those restaurants run less on the conveyor-belt principle – the food might even taste better.

Liquids

A combination of low humidity in the aircraft and often high ambient temperatures on the ground, means that pilots must keep their bodies well topped-up with fluids. This is not always as straightforward as it might appear, because:

(a) Large quantities of any one drink (tea, coffee etc.) may cause indigestion or other side-effects.

(b) Carbonated drinks can cause discomfort due to the low cabin pressure encouraging the release of CO_2 in the alimentary canal.

(c) Most soft drinks contain undesirably high concentrations of sugar.

(d) of the often unpleasant taste of aircraft water.

The answer may be to 'mix your drinks', or, in extreme circumstances, insist on bottled water.

Hygiene

Food hygiene, both in the air and on the ground, is not always as good as it ought to be. With the possibility of mass crew incapacitation in mind, it is therefore important for pilots to eat different meals, not only in flight, but also immediately prior to going on duty. The more acute forms of food poisoning usually produce symptoms within six hours, so some relaxation of this rule is permissable outside this period. Particular care should be taken when eating seafood, salads, artificial cream, and trifle-type desserts. Undercooked meat may also be hazardous in certain parts of the world. This subject is discussed in more detail in the chapter on tropical hygiene.

4 Sleep Guidance

Nature and function of sleep

Sleep is a fundamental necessity of life. Normal orthodox sleep can be divided into four recognisable stages of brain and bodily activity; stage one being the lightest, through to stage four, the deepest sleep. During a normal uninterrupted night's sleep, there are about thirty spontaneous changes from one stage to another. There is also another type of sleep, called paradoxical sleep or REM (from Rapid Eye Movement) – a characteristic feature. There is marked brain and body activity during these periods of paradoxical sleep, which occur on four or five occasions during a normal night's rest, and occupy about one fifth of the total time asleep. It is then that dreaming takes place. Both types of sleep are essential, and it is thought that restoration of body tissues occurs during orthodox sleep, while the function of paradoxical sleep is the maintainance and repair of brain cells.

Sleep deprivation

In commercial aviation, with aircraft utilised round the clock, sleep disturbance for aircrew is inevitable. Cumulative sleep deprivation can build up on certain adverse tours of duty, when the total amount of sleep achieved by an individual, averaged over the length of the tour, falls below that individual's normal average night's sleep. To offset this type of cumulative deprivation, attempt where practical and possible to obtain the extra sleep necessary to bring the average sleep over the tour up to normal levels, either by additional 'naps' or by sleeping-in longer. Recommendations to help maximise sleep are:

(a) A quiet, adequately-ventilated, heavily-curtained room with a firm, comfortable bed.

(b) Ensure adequate physical activity during waking hours.

(c) Avoid stimulants (coffee, tea etc.) prior to sleeping.

(d) Avoid stress-inducing activities immediately prior to sleeping.

Owing to the essential function of sleep, it is unlikely that long-term sleep deprivation would reach dangerous levels, because when the body really needs sleep, it will take it, even if it means falling asleep in the most unlikely places. However, operating under conditions of short-term sleep loss is a common problem for aircrew.

Human performance deteriorates with sleep loss. The deterioration is greater in tasks requiring self-generated arousal, such as system monitoring. The reason is that sleep loss will cause a reduction in the motivation to perform a task even though the capacity to perform that task may be little altered. Furthermore, under these conditions, whilst it is possible to raise performance for a while, it requires extra effort, and cannot be sustained for long. A disturbing feature of the inconsistencies in performance and lapses in alertness associated with sleep loss, is that the subject is not normally conscious of his deteriorating performance. Hence the importance of a fuller understanding of the subject by aircrew.

Body rhythms

Most of the chemical and some physical processes of the body occur in regular cycles. Whilst there are faster and slower measurable cycles, by far the most common is the twenty-four hour cycle or circadian rhythm.

It is the interaction of the various processes during their circadian cycles that produces the peak of performance during the day, and allows rest and sleep at night. The rhythms vary from one individual to another, accounting for the so-called phenomenon of 'morning people' and 'evening people', depending upon the time of day of the individual's performance peak. The circadian rhythms are normally rigidly synchronised by external cues such as light, dark, the clock and various social factors, which are all given the name zeitgebers. Hence by shifting the zeitgebers (for example, moving to a different time zone) a shift of the body rhythms occurs in order to re-synchronise with the new time. Most rhythms will shift at a rate of about one and a half hours every day, but some change at slower rates, down to only half an hour per day. This means there is an initial period when the various circadian rhythms are de-synchronised, and in the most adverse cases it can take up to three weeks before all the processes have fully readjusted to the new time. Hence, the body systems of some of the long-range flight crews may never be allowed any stabilisation throughout their whole flying career (with the possible exception of annual leave and technical courses).

Since the biochemical processes are intimately related to the sleep patterns, it follows that disturbance of one will upset the other. Thus, time zone change will give rise to sleep disturbance and below par bodily function; likewise, sleep disruption by night-flying will lead to similar disorders. It is a hard fact of airline life that these disruptions will occur, but it is as well for the individual to be aware of them and try, where possible, to mitigate the effects. There is likely to be a physical penalty associated with the continual disturbance of circadian rhythms, and it has been suggested that a link exists with certain ailments such as stomach and bowel disorders. Psychologically, there is variation in performance associated with these disturbances, allied with the normal variation in performance depending upon the time of day.

Performance deterioration

The previously-mentioned deterioration in performance due to sleep loss is further compounded by the variations caused by disturbance of circadian rhythms. In order to minimise these effects on the flight deck:

(a) Keep workload within every crew member's capability. Expect some mistakes and errors, and be meticulous in cross checks and double checks.

(b) Do not place too much reliance on the memory – be more inclined to refer to the paperwork and manuals for information, and write down all instructions straight away to prevent them being forgotten.

(c) Be aware that not only is physical and mental performance likely to be below par, but also there may be inadequate recognition of this deteriorating performance. So make the operation as simple, standard and unhurried as is possible:
    (i) Do not take short cuts that will cause extra workload.
    (ii) Use all the aids and automatics to the full where this makes the task easier.
    (iii) Adhere firmly to standard operating procedures – do not rush yourself, or allow others to rush you.

Pre-flight sleep

Whether on long-range transmeridian duties, or a tour of night-flying in and out of base, the aim is to achieve a healthy sleep prior to going on duty. Since the body rhythms play a large part in this, any answer will usually vary from one individual to another. However, a working knowledge of the principles involved, coupled with experience of the duty patterns, should assist in finding the optimum solution.

A. SLEEP/WAKEFULNESS INTERACTION
A normal night's sleep of (say) eight hours will give a 'sleep credit in the store' of (say) sixteen hours potential wakefulness, and after a normal sixteen hour day of work plus recreation, the 'sleep store' will be down to zero. At this time the normal man retires to sleep and the process begins again. This can be visualised as a saw tooth pattern, as shown in the diagram overleaf:
    There are certain principles which can be derived:

(a) A full eight hour sleep follows a normal period awake of sixteen hours. If the period of wakefulness is significantly foreshortened, then a good sleep is unlikely while there is still 'credit in the sleepstore'.

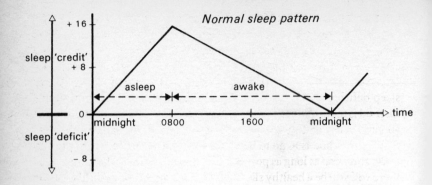

Normal sleep pattern

(b) If the length of the sleep period is reduced, the length of the following period of useful wakefulness before feeling tired is also reduced.

(c) Following any period of wakefulness greater than sixteen hours, some sleep should be possible, since the 'sleep store is in deficit'.

B. THE 'BODY CLOCK'

The various circadian rhythms, synchronised by the zeitgebers, ensure that the normal man is tired enough to sleep from (say) midnight until 8 a.m., and he is awake and alert to carry out his work and recreation from 8 a.m. to midnight. The slow rate of change of the circadian rhythms, following a shift of zeitgebers, means that the sleep/wakefulness cycle of the 'body clock' is geared fairly closely to time at home base during a short tour of duty, irrespective of the sleep/work patterns.

Thus, even following a long duty, sleep is likely to be poor if it occurs during the 'body clock's' day. Similarly, tiredness is likely to be felt if working during the 'body clock's' night, even though a good pre-duty sleep was obtained.

When large time changes are involved during a tour of duty, the zeitgebers will be gradually aligning the circadian rhythms towards the new time zone. If several days are spent in or around the same time zone, then the 'body clock' can often conveniently be considered to be moving away from base time at an hour or so per day.

C. NIGHT-FLYING FROM BASE

Perhaps one of the most difficult pre-flight sleeps to achieve is that before night-flying from base. One method is to foreshorten the previous night's sleep by rising early in the morning (hence gaining a smaller than normal sleep store credit) and going to bed again in the early evening (when the sleep store is back down to zero) and obtaining several hours of sleep prior to duty. The big disadvantage is that, should other factors prevent further sleep, duty would start with an even larger sleep deficit than otherwise. Taking body rhythms into account, this method is more likely to be successful for the individual who is normally an early riser, and whose performance peak comes early in the day. Another method is to go to bed later than normal on the night prior to duty, and sleep as long as possible into the day. Thus at the start of duty there will still be a healthy sleep credit. This method is more likely to be successful for the normally late riser whose performance peak occurs later in the day.

D. NIGHT-FLYING AWAY FROM BASE
Obtaining some pre-flight sleep is likely to be less of a problem provided time changes of the order of several hours are involved. West of base the 'body clock's night' will coincide more with the late afternoon to evening of the station, assisting in obtaining sleep at that time. East of base the 'body clock's' night coincides more with the morning to early afternoon of the station, assisting in sleeping-in late on the day prior to the night duty.

E. THE TWENTY-FOUR HOUR REST PERIOD
This commonly becomes a problem following a long, tiring duty, since sleep of a good eight hours or more is probable straight away, thus meaning no more sleep is likely until it is time to go on duty again, because the sleep store is well in credit. The choice is usually whether to curtail the post-flight sleep by an early alarm call, with the expectancy of obtaining a few hours sleep prior to the next duty, or to delay the first sleep as long as possible, and hope to sleep late. Resolution of this dilemma must depend on other considerations, such as:

(a) The relationship between the duty schedule and local night time; a long sleep is usually more likely during the local night than during the local day.

(b) Where a large time change has occurred be aware of the relationship between the duty schedule and local time at base. Body rhythms can play a part here and allow a long sleep if it is taken over the period of night time at home (the body clock's night).

31

F. SOPORIFICS

The arrangement of duty is clearly most important, but some aircrew, as they grow older, find it increasingly difficult to cope with irregularity of rest. Indeed, irregularity of rest superimposed upon the less restful sleep of middle age can be very troublesome, and in middle age you must look after your sleep. Exercise and avoiding heavy meals as well as limiting or even avoiding the use of alcohol, nicotine and caffeine will help. You should also consider less demanding routes. However, if difficulties with your sleep persist after attention to these matters a discussion with your flight medical officer could be most useful. There is now much greater understanding of sleep disturbance, and the doctor will make sure, first of all, that there is no medical reason for your problem.

With attention to your style of life and in the absence of any medical problem which could lead to disturbed sleep, the doctor may feel that the occasional use of an hypnotic could be of benefit. However, it is important that the choice of hypnotic is free of unwanted effects during the next duty period. Current experience suggests that temazepam (Normison – Wyeth: 10–20 mg) is the drug of choice for aircrew. It has a short duration of action, but it should be used 'on the ground' before it is prescribed during a schedule. It should be given at the lowest dose and then as infrequently as possible, and you should identify the one or two occasions during a schedule when it is likely to be of most benefit. In general, there should be an interval of 24 hours between ingestion and commencement of duty, though with medical advice the interval can be reduced to 12 hours. Perhaps it is unnecessary to emphasise that if you use hypnotics alcohol should be severely limited and preferably avoided.

5 Some Aspects of Aviation Physiology

(or what is lying in wait for the healthy man in the aviation environment).

Hypoxia

Lack of oxygen is probably the greatest single danger of high altitude flight. In spite of its rarity, it merits special consideration as not everyone has had the advantage of a practical demonstration of the symptoms in a decompression chamber. Up to 10,000 feet cabin altitude, the effects of oxygen lack are barely noticeable in the healthy pilot. Above 10,000 feet, and up to around 18,000 feet cabin altitude, the symptoms of hypoxia become more intrusive although there are compensatory actions of quicker breathing and faster heartbeat giving increased blood flow to the brain. Above 18,000 feet, hypoxia will eventually lead to irrationality and then unconsciousness. The time of useful consciousness reduces rapidly from around ten minutes at 20,000 feet to a couple of minutes at 25,000 feet; until above 30,000 feet when it is *less than thirty seconds*.

The first symptoms of hypoxia may be misleadingly pleasant; a euphoria resembling mild intoxication. Since the brain is the prime target for oxygen starvation, it is the higher faculties that are dulled first; the mind no longer works properly or self-critically, and there is a false sense of security. The hands and feet become clumsy without your being aware of it, and you may feel drowsy, languid and nonchalant. As the hypoxia worsens, there may be feelings of giddiness, tingling of the skin and dull aches in the head. By now the heart is racing, the lips and fingernails begin to turn blue and the field of vision narrows. Finally there are muscle spasms, unco-ordinated movements of the limbs, visual and auditory failure and semi-consciousness, leading to unconsciousness. Ironically, throughout all this you feel confident that you are performing better than ever and are totally unaware of your failing faculties. Because of its self-deceiving nature, the only way of avoiding hypoxia is to prevent it before it starts. This means, if the cabin altitude starts an unscheduled climb – GET ON OXYGEN, and *stay* on it until the cabin altitude is back down below 10,000 feet.

Loss of pressurisation

This is, of course, closely linked to the above section on hypoxia. Whilst we are all required to memorise and practice the drills associated with loss of pressurisation and emergency descent, it may be useful to cover the events that are likely to be experienced in the most severe type of rapid loss of pressurisation in the aircraft.

The following, for all practical purposes, occur simultaneously:

(a) A loud startling noise, (caused by cabin air leaving the aircraft at speeds up to, or greater than, the speed of sound).

(b) Dense fogging due to condensation of moisture, which rapidly clears as (c) occurs.

(c) A very strong and sudden rush of wind. This causes dust and loose articles to fly around the cockpit and cabin.

(d) Sudden and extreme drop in temperature.

(e) Sudden feeling of chest expansion followed instantly by forced exhalation.

(f) Severe pain in the ears and abdomen accompanied by a release of wind.

These are, to say the least, startling events. However, there is no time to waste, since at current cruising levels, particularly above 30,000 feet, you have *literally* a matter of seconds to **PUT ON YOUR OXYGEN MASK INSTANTLY AND TIGHTLY** and then begin the **EMERGENCY DESCENT.** *Remember*, you will not be able to put on your mask once past the period of useful consciousness, nor will other crew members be able to safely help you. Apart from the obvious danger to the aircraft, prolonged hypoxia, under these conditions, can cause permanent brain damage. Even in a slow decompression, some of the above events may be noticed to a lesser degree but the priority is *always* to put on your oxygen mask. Never try to hold your breath in a decompression; this could cause damage to your lungs.

Decompression sickness (the 'bends')

This condition is due to nitrogen dissolved in the tissue fluids forming gaseous bubbles under reduced atmospheric pressure. It is likely to happen only while flying shortly after sub-aqua diving. Do not fly within forty-eight hours of diving to depths greater than thirty-three feet (Two Atmospheres Absolute).

Susceptibility to decompression sickness is increased with advancing age, obesity, fatigue and alcohol intake. Re-exposure to the compression/decompression cycle will increase the likelihood of its occurrence, as will exercise. The parts most involved in diving (shoulder, upper arm muscles and associated joints) are the sites most likely for symptoms of the condition, which are stiffness in the joints and rheumatic-like pains in the muscles. There could also be a painful choking feeling, tingling sensations and paralysis. If symptoms do appear, descent to a lower cabin altitude *must be made*. After landing, medical advice should be sought. The prevention and treatment should be taken seriously, *for death may follow apparently trivial episodes*.

Hyperventilation

Before leaving the subject of respiration, a few words on hyperventilation. This is 'over-breathing', usually caused by anxiety, excitement or fear.

The symptoms are similar to those of hypoxia, with numbness, giddiness and tingling of the face and limbs, accompanied by gasping for air. If the breathing is not brought under control by conscious effort, then hyperventilation can lead to blurring of vision, muscle spasms and unconsciousness. This subject is also covered under First Aid on page 63 of the handbook.

Vertigo, giddiness and motion sickness

Simple giddiness or dizziness is a symptom of, amongst other things, oxygen imbalance in the brain, as has been mentioned previously. However, vertigo is a definite feeling of rotation, brought about by disease, or over-stimulation of the sensory organs by rapid accelerations. (It is the sensation you can experience after spinning rapidly on the spot.) It may even occur suddenly whilst blowing the nose or sneezing, due to a violent change of air pressure transmitted to the middle ear, disturbing the balance mechanisms of the inner ear and feeding conflicting messages to the brain.

Motion sickness is also related to over-stimulation of the sensory perceptors, made worse by the fear of the thought of being sick. Air-sickness drugs all have side reactions; in particular they induce drowsiness. Whilst flying, such drugs should only be taken under *strict medical supervision*.

Spatial disorientation

This is subtly different from the above, in that it is an illusion of position, attitude or movement in space, *without* accompanying giddiness, vertigo or nausea. It occurs when the perception of orientation is distorted by acceleration forces whilst true visual reference has been lost. The semi-circular canals of the inner ear send distorted messages to the brain, when subjected to the accelerations of flight, as do the various physical pressure points throughout the body which make up its balance mechanism, known as 'seat-of-the-pants', which themselves can also be fairly insensitive to gradual changes and small accelerations. Disorientation is more likely to occur in visual flight because of the characteristics of swept-wing jet transports, smooth, constant noise levels, lack of genuine 'feel', high angular accelerations due to the cockpit being so far ahead of the centre of gravity and the inability to see the wings peripherally as a basic visual reference. The likelihood of spatial disorientation is increased in poor visibility and lighting conditions, and if suffering from the effects of fatigue, minor illness or boredom.

So, if you experience disorientation, *get back on instruments and evaluate them before taking any corrective action.* Consider handing over control to the other pilot. Remember that it sometimes requires a great mental effort to disregard these false sensory images and to believe the instruments.

Visual illusions

These can be considered as a type of spatial disorientation, this time due to false sensory inputs from the usually reliable source of the eyes, caused by optical illusions. Awareness of the possibility of visual illusions, reference to the instruments and full use of available approach aids are the best preventive measures.

(a) *Sloping Approach Terrain:* Up or down slope of the terrain to the runway threshold causing an above or below glide slope illusion respectively.

(b) *Sloping Runway:* Up or down slope of the runway itself causing an above or below glide slope illusion respectively.

(c) *Runway Width:* The greater the width of a runway, the shorter the runway length appears, and the lower the aircraft appears to be, from the same relative position on the approach.

(d) *Runway Lights:* Bright or dim runway lighting causes the runway to seem closer or further away respectively.

(e) *Restricted Visibility:* Poor visibility causes the illusion of being higher than normal due to the absence of shadows aiding depth perception. This illusion may also be encountered during approaches over smooth water.

(f) *Windscreen Refraction:* Heavy rain on the windscreen can cause refraction giving rise to an illusion of being off the glidescope or localiser, or both.

(g) *Auto-kinetic Illusion:* A point source of light viewed against a featureless background at night will appear to oscillate, with the amplitude increasing if the object is allowed to become the prime focus of attention.

(h) *Octogyral Illusion:* The apparent movement of a light source at night, viewed during a manoeuvre involving considerable angular acceleration, which may continue after resuming straight and level flight.

(i) *The 'Upside-down' Illusion:* Can occur in conditions of high altitude in extreme darkness with no stars or other visual clues above the aircraft, and the moon seen below the aircraft.

Severe turbulence

Moderate to severe turbulence can adversely affect the performance of the human pilot in the following ways:

(a) Decision time is increased.

(b) There is a likelihood of 'control reversal' (consciously making control inputs in the wrong direction, especially during negative G).

(c) Tendency to over-control.

(d) Involuntary control actions occur without being obvious.

(e) Transient blurring of vision and difficulty in maintaining focus on the instruments (particularly during negative G).

(f) The sensory mechanisms are deceived.

Luckily the autopilot suffers from none of these effects. However, if you have to hand-fly during severe turbulence, the following advice may help:

(a) Wear full harness, well tightened and push yourself back into the seat.

(b) Try to ignore the inputs from the 'seat-of-the-pants' and inner ear mechanisms; concentrate primarily on the artificial horizon (often wrong and misleading information can be given by the altimeter, VSI and ASI). Beware of natural reactions to the positive and negative G forces.

(c) Be aware that moderate turbulence can suddenly increase to unusually severe intensity, and be mentally prepared for such an eventuality.

6 Further Aspects of Aviation Physiology

Up to now we have discussed the adverse effects of the aviation environment on the healthy pilot. There are, however, further considerations if the pilot is suffering from ill health.

Heart disease

This highly complex subject is of particular importance. It is the most frequent cause of death in the UK amongst men of working age, and is our number one cause of loss of licence. Many different disease processes can damage the heart and blood vessels (the cardiovascular system). There is enormous variation amongst individuals as to the speed and manner in which the disease progresses. It ranges from the sudden death of a person who was apparently in excellent health, through those suffering from a variety of chest pains and heart attacks, to people who live for many productive years, yet with obvious manifestations of the disease.

Coronary arteries, the blood vessels that feed the heart, are particularly vulnerable to atherosclerosis. This 'hardening of the arteries' is the gradual building up of deposits on the inside of the arterial wall. These deposits contain a high proportion of fats and cholesterol and the process is very slow, often starting during the 'teens'. If a coronary artery eventually becomes sufficiently narrowed by deposits, a blood clot (or thrombus) can block the artery. This coronary thrombosis causes the heart muscle supplied by that artery to be starved of food and oxygen, and the muscle ceases to work, giving rise to a 'heart attack', or myocardial infarction. The severity of the attack depends upon the degree of impairment of the heart's function. The affected heart muscle usually causes electrical changes in the heart, and these will show up on the electrocardiograph (ECG). Angina, or chest pains after exertion, are similarly caused by inadequate blood supply to the heart muscle.

The cause of heart disease is not known. However, there are certain predisposing factors which strongly indicate a greater chance of suffering from heart disease in later life. These risk factors are:

(a) Family history of coronary heart disease, strokes and high blood pressure.

(b) Hypertension – high blood pressure.

(c) Cigarette smoking.

(d) Lack of exercise.

(c) Diabetes.

(f) Obesity.

(g) Hyperlipidaemia – elevated blood cholesterol and blood lipid levels.

(h) Stress.

A. FAMILY HISTORY

There appears to be a hereditary influence in the development of heart disease. However, should your family have a history of coronary heart disease, strokes or high blood pressure, this on its own is no cause for concern, provided other risk factors are not present. If they are present, then more urgency is required in avoiding or controlling them. All other risk factors can be reduced by taking the necessary action and modifying your life-style where possible.

B. HYPERTENSION
High blood pressure is a significant cause of loss of licence in its own right, apart from its link with heart disease. Its control requires long term co-operation with your doctor. Often a change in diet, a reduction in weight, taking up exercise, or cutting down smoking, can corrrect moderately elevated blood pressure. More serious cases require the use of drugs. It is possible in certain cases to retain your licence whilst undergoing drug therapy, operating under a waiver from the aviation authority.

C. CIGARETTE SMOKING
The nicotine in cigarette smoke affects the heart. The carbon monoxide in cigarette smoke reduces the transport of oxygen in the blood. If you smoke, you more than *double* the risk of developing heart disease, apart from the damage it does to your lungs!

There is really only one useful piece of advice about smoking – DON'T! Giving up smoking is not an easy task, but the benefits are enormous, both in increased longevity and improved physical fitness. Cutting down on cigarettes, or switching to a pipe or cigars may help, but it is far better, if possible, to give up smoking entirely. Even those who have smoked for many years will, if they give up, rapidly reduce their risk of having a coronary attack. It is always worth stopping smoking, but better never to start.

D. LACK OF EXERCISE
Inactivity is directly linked to increased risk of heart disease. The virtues of physical fitness and exercise have already been described in chapter 1. However, it is here worth emphasising the warning against sudden bursts of strenuous exercise after long periods of inactivity; remember, it is regular, moderate exercise which will help to prevent heart disease.

E. DIABETES
As well as increasing the likelihood of heart disease, diabetes is a disorder that can lead to licence loss in its own right. The cause of the disease is largely unknown, but it results in the pancreas producing

insufficient insulin. This is required by the body cells in the utilisation of sugar for energy, and when insulin is lacking, the cells use other compounds instead of sugar. This gives rise to byproducts that are toxic to the body, and produces the signs and symptoms of diabetes, such as persistent tiredness and slow reactions. A frequent factor in diabetes is over-eating sugar products, also being overweight.

If detected early by a glucose tolerance test, mild diabetes can often be controlled with a carefully balanced diet, weight loss and exercise. More advanced cases require regular doses of insulin.

F. OBESITY

Obesity indicates an increased risk of heart disease as well as leading to hypertension, diabetes and a general decrease in life expectancy!

Your desirable weight can be found in the table opposite, recommended by the Royal College of Physicians. For most people this should be about the weight you were when at the peak of physical fitness in your early twenties.

Losing weight, and keeping weight down is simply a matter of eating less. This does not mean a crash starvation diet, but a gradual overall reduction in the amount eaten. Follow the advice given in chapter 3, cut down on starchy and fatty foods, and concentrate more on proteins and green vegetables. Remember, as you lose weight you will not only improve your health and feel better, but you will look better as well.

G. HYPERLIPIDAEMIA

Cholesterol is a fatty substance used in metabolism, both produced in the liver and derived from the diet (from foods such as meat, shellfish, dairy produce and eggs). It is transported through the blood in combination with complex blood proteins known as lipoproteins. Adverse high concentrations of these various substances can result in atherosclerosis. A blood test will show if the levels of these substances are elevated and changes in diet will be recommended by the doctor to control them. As a general guide for all of us, dietary fat should contribute less than a third of the total calorie intake. It is advisable to restrict the consumption of all fats, particularly saturated fats, from meat and dairy produce. Substitution with polyunsaturated fats (such as corn oil) may help.

H. STRESS

Those in 'high stress' occupations are reckoned to be more at risk from

Desirable weight of adults according to height and frame. Based on weights of insured persons in the USA associated with lowest mortality (Macleod, 1974).

Height without shoes			Desirable weight in kilograms and pounds (in indoor clothing), ages 25 and over					
			small frame		Medium frame		Large frame	
metres	ft	in	kg	lb	kg	lb	kg	lb

Men

metres	ft	in	kg	lb	kg	lb	kg	lb
1.550	5	1	50.8-54.4	112-120	53.5-58.5	118-129	57.2-64	126-141
1.575	5	2	52.5-55.8	115-123	54.9-60.3	121-133	58.5-65.3	129-144
1.600	5	3	53.5-57.2	118-126	56.2-56.7	124-136	59.9-67.1	132-148
1.625	5	4	54.9-58.5	121-129	57.6-63	127-139	61.2-68.9	135-152
1.650	5	5	56.2-60.3	124-133	59 -64.9	130-143	62.6-70.8	138-156
1.675	5	6	58.1-62.1	128-137	60.8-66.7	134-147	64.4-73	142-161
1.700	5	7	59.9-64	132-141	62.6-68.9	138-152	66.7-75.3	147-166
1.725	5	8	61.7-65.8	136-145	64.4-70.8	142-156	68.5-77.1	151-170
1.750	5	9	63.5-68	140-150	66.2-72.6	146-160	70.3-78.9	155-174
1.775	5	10	65.3-69.9	144-154	68 -74.8	150-165	72.1-81.2	159-179
1.800	5	11	67.1-71.7	148-158	69.9-77.1	154-170	74.4-83.5	164-184
1.825	6	0	68.9-73.5	152-162	71.7-79.4	158-175	76.2-85.7	168-189
1.850	6	1	70.8-75.7	156-167	73.5-81.6	162-180	78.5-88	173-194
1.875	6	2	72.6-77.6	160-171	75.7-83.9	167-185	80.7-90.3	178-199
1.900	6	3	74.4-79.4	164-175	78.0-86.2	172-190	82.6-92.5	182-204

Women

metres	ft	in	kg	lb	kg	lb	kg	lb
1.425	4	8	41.7-44.5	92-98	43.5-48.5	96-107	47.2-54	104-119
1.450	4	9	42.6-45.8	94-101	44.5-49.9	98-110	48.1-55.3	106-122
1.475	4	10	43.5-47.2	96-104	45.8-51.3	101-113	49.4-56.7	109-125
1.500	4	11	44.9-48.5	99-107	47.2-52.6	104-116	50.8-58.1	112-128
1.525	5	0	46.3-49.9	102-110	48.5-54	107-119	52.5-59.4	115-131
1.550	5	1	47.6-51.3	105-113	49.9-55.3	110-122	53.5-60.8	118-134
1.575	5	2	49 -52.6	108-116	51.3-57.2	113-126	54.9-62.6	121-138
1.600	5	3	50.3-54	111-119	52.6-59	116-130	56.7-64.4	125-142
1.625	5	4	51.7-55.8	114-123	54.4-61.2	120-135	58.5-66.2	129-146
1.650	5	5	53.5-57.6	118-127	56.2-63	124-139	60.3-68	133-150
1.675	5	6	55.3-59.4	122-131	58.1-64.9	128-143	62.1-69.9	137-154
1.700	5	7	57.2-61.2	126-135	59.9-66.7	132-147	64 -71.7	141-158
1.725	5	8	59 -63.5	130-140	61.7-68.5	136-151	65.8-73.9	145-163
1.750	5	9	60.8-65.3	134-144	63.5-70.3	140-155	67.6-76.2	149-168
1.775	5	10	62.6-67.1	138-148	65.3-72.1	144-159	69.4-78.5	153-173

Source: Page 31 of a Report on the Prevention of Coronary Heart Disease, produced by a joint Working Party of the Royal College of Physicians, London and the British Cardiac Society, reprinted from the Journal of the RCP, Vol. 10, No. 3, April 1976.

heart attacks. The subject of stress is fully discussed in chapter 3; suffice it to say here that, if you have been overdoing it with things getting on top of you, relaxation and 'getting away from it all' will not only help you psychologically – your heart will benefit as well.

Hence, by recognising the presence of any of the risk factors, and taking simple, positive steps to control them you will greatly reduce the chances of heart disease, losing your licence or even losing your life.

Backache

Backache is a serious problem among pilots. The backbone is a complex structure and may be injured in many ways, although the common factor is excess loading exacerbated by poorly designed seating. The way to keep one's back in good condition is relatively simple. On the aircraft get out of the seat to move about as often as possible, at least every hour – more if possible. This is thought to increase circulation to the spine and to relieve pressure on the 'discs'; it may also relieve aching muscles. Most aircraft seats offer little support to the small of the back which allows one to slump in the seat. This is not a good thing since it increases pressure within the invertebral discs which may in time contribute towards their degeneration and subsequent chronic backache. Proper support in the small of the back may also relieve aching muscles. How much support is necessary will vary between individuals. Where it becomes crucial to have good support to relieve pain, individually-made, moulded-plastic lumbar cushions are available (Institute of Aviation Medicine and British Airways produce personal cushions). Others are available commercially. Following a long flight, some light exercise, such as walking, is far better for you than slumping in an easy chair.

'The other necessity for keeping a fit back is to exercise sufficiently to keep the back's supporting muscles strong enough to do their job, which is to stabilise the column of vertebrae rather like the mast of a sailing ship is strengthened by its stays. In a fit person the curvature of the spine is continually altered during movement to maintain the geometry so that loads are transmitted with least danger of damage. Bending forward, however, induces the muscles to relax so that lifting weights from the floor can more easily cause damage if you fail to bend at the knees and lift with a straight back (the muscles then contract instead of relaxing, and spinal damage is unlikely.)'

'Having disposed of the fit, a few words to those who already suffer backache. Recent work has shown that most backache is a symptom of structural distress

44

of some part of the spine, which is a remarkably complex piece of engineering. Methods of diagnosing exactly what is causing pain have recently improved, e.g. stereo x-ray techniques have shown previously undetectable fractures of the vertebrae. One common but misnamed ailment is worthy of mention – the slipped disc. It is often assumed that a disc "slips" due to some unusually severe action or jar – this is not so. A disc does not slip, it bursts, and will only rupture if it is already degenerate. If a healthy disc is greatly overloaded it may rupture eventually but in a different manner. It may be some comfort to those who develop sciatica due to a prolapsed disc after exercise, to know that the disc was previously abnormal, and exercise only precipitated an event which probably would have occurred anyway.'

'Pressure within a disc is least on reclining but increases with standing, sitting, leaning forward and lifting. There are changes of pressure with good and bad sitting postures and with or without lumbar support which can be related to the comfort of sitting. The degenerate disc nucleus does not transmit pressures in the same way as a normal nucleus so that increased loads fall upon other parts of the structure. This in turn may lead to micro-fractures of the vertebral end-plates and greater stress on the outer annulus fibrosus of the disc, thus exacerbating disc damage and possibly causing backache.

To summarise:
Backache is an occupational hazard but not inevitable. A little thought and some simple precautions will help you avoid it.

(a) DON'T SIT WITH A SAGGING BACK. Where possible sit in seats that give a good posture, preferably with knees higher than hips.

(b) DON'T SIT FOR PROLONGED PERIODS in one seat or one position. This is most important in the prevention of circulatory disorders as well as backache.

(c) TAKE REGULAR EXERCISE. Some sports are especially good for maintaining muscular fitness in the back (e.g. backstroke swimming). The Appendix on page 76 gives exercises specifically designed to strengthen back muscles.

(d) DON'T STOOP OR LIFT HEAVY OBJECTS AT ARMS' LENGTH – BEND YOUR KNEES. Use common sense when digging or performing other strenuous jobs that put an extra load on the back. Keep it STRAIGHT AND PERPENDICULAR, and if you do hurt your back *don't carry on – rest it*. It is then that the risk of more serious injury is highest.

(e) Finally, if you are suffering from acute pain in the back then THE BEST CURE IS REST. Severe or prolonged attacks should ALWAYS be referred to a doctor.

Hypoglycaemia

This condition is one in which the sugar content of the blood has fallen to a dangerously low level. Symptoms may include lassitude and drowsiness or light-headedness, and ultimately even collapse and unconsciousness. More significant however, the brain and nervous systems are amongst the first affected, and there is a noticeable irascibility, falling-off in the ability to exercise judgement and to make decisions.

It can occur as a result of disease, or of an insulin overdose in a diabetic; more significantly, it may occur in a healthy individual who has been without sustenance for several hours and is suddenly subject to mental anxiety or physical exercise. Coupled with disturbance of the circadian rhythms associated with the digestion and absorption of food, hypoglycaemia is a definite hazard to the professional pilot.

DO NOT 'skip' meals whilst flying: in particular, **ENSURE YOU EAT A MEAL IMMEDIATELY PRIOR TO COMMENCING DUTY.** Remember also, a quick booster can be obtained if necessary by drinking sweet drinks.

Common congestive disorders

INFLAMMATION OF THE MIDDLE AND INNER EAR

The middle ear is an air-filled cavity, connected to the space behind the nose (the naso-pharynx) by the Eustachian tube. Air pressure is thus equalised on both sides of the ear drum. The mucous membrane lining the Eustachian tube is set in folds, acting similarly to a non-return valve, making it more difficult for air to enter the middle ear than to leave it. Hence, if any problems occur with equalisation of air pressure through inflammation of the ear (otitis), it will be more noticeable on the descent.

COMMON COLD, SINUSITIS, TONSILLITIS

Any infection or allergic condition capable of causing catarrh or swelling of the tissues in and around the Eustachian tubes, can give rise to 'blocked ears'. Should problems occur in flight, try yawning, swallowing, 'clearing the ears' (by pinching the nose and blowing), or sniffing proprietary decongestants. Inability to equalise the air pressure will distort the eardrum, cause very severe pain and could later give rise to infection. If the condition persists after landing, *see a doctor*. The most serious cases will lead to rupture of the eardrum (otitic barotrauma) with a consequent long period of grounding for medical treatment. Subsequent infection and deafness are possible.

SINUS BAROTRAUMA

The cavities in the bone of the skull (paranasal sinuses) are connected to the nasal cavities by tubes, and with certain disorders (for example, common cold, hay fever) these may become blocked, in a manner similar to the Eustachian tubes. Consequent pressure differences may cause intense pain in the forehead and eyes, headache and watering of the eyes. Grounding is necessary until treatment is effective.

The message is clear; if you have a cold, sore throat, catarrh, hay fever or any other similar condition and, especially if you cannot clear your ears, **DO NOT FLY.** The risk is simply not worth it.

Mild oxygen deficiency

Apart from hypoxia, discussed in chapter 5, milder oxygen deficiency can also be troublesome and even dangerous, causing fatigue, lethargy and slow reaction. Associated causal factors are high cabin altitude, smoking, obesity, overtiredness and lack of movement causing reduced blood circulation. Oxygen deficiency can be dangerous in that the brain may not recognise the condition, being itself affected. Frequent yawning is common. The solution is obvious; take a walk around occasionally, reduce or stop smoking, and if necessary use oxygen.

Hearing impairment

With the advent of modern aeroplanes and VHF radio, the noise levels in headphones and the background noise have become more acceptable, and hearing impairment due to flying is not so frequent. However, hearing impairment is inevitable with advancing age, particularly in the high frequency range. Although such impairment is usually not a significant problem when flying, it is sensible not to abuse one's ears, which will stand occasional high noise levels without permanent damage, but regular exposure to very noisy situations can lead to early deafness.

Obviously, whilst one cannot be expected to wear earmuffs in a disco, precautions can be taken now and then. If one pursues a noisy hobby such as shooting or model aircraft flying, the use of earplugs would be prudent.

Visual standards

These are, of course, fully tested at every licence medical but a plain language explanation of the principles involved may well be useful.

Visual acuity (the ability to see), is assessed by the use of a Sneller's Test Card, viewed from a distance of six metres. Depending on the line of letters that can be read, vision is recorded as a fraction. Thus the required minimum standard for the professional pilot of 6/9 means the eye, at a distance of six metres from the card, can only read the larger letters intended to be read by the normal eye at a distance of nine metres. (The standard for the unaided eye may be as low as 6/18, provided it can be corrected to 6/9 with glasses.)

LONG SIGHT (HYPERMETROPIA)
This occurs where parallel light rays enter the fully relaxed eye to come to a focus *behind* the retina. This would be corrected, where necessary, with glasses having a convex lens. Presbyopia is long-sightedness, usually noticed in the early forties, which is caused by changes, through age, in the substance of the lens in the eye. This, although quite normal, causes the lens to lose some of its elasticity and hence be less able to accommodate extreme ranges of vision. This will require glasses for close work or reading.

SHORT SIGHT (MYOPIA)
In this case the light rays are focused *in front of* the retina of the fully relaxed eye and the correction will be made, if necessary, with a concave lens.

ASTIGMATISM
This relates to abnormalities of the curvature of the surface of the cornea and the surface of the lens. The healthy cornea is spherically shaped, whereas the astigmatic cornea is oval shaped. The consequent errors of refraction are corrected by a cylindrical lens.

OCULAR MUSCLE BALANCE
The various muscles of the eye are co-ordinated by a complex neuro-muscular mechanism which results in the visual axes of both eyes being directed towards the focus of attention. Heterophoria is that condition of the eyes in which the visual axes fail to maintain their normal direction when the stimulus of binocular vision is temporarily

removed. This results in convergence (esophoria), divergence (exophoria) or vertical deviation either up or down (hyperphoria or hypophoria). These states constitute the various forms of latent squint (strabismus) and are important in that they may give rise to blurring of vision, headaches or double vision, particularly noticeable when tired.

NIGHT VISION
Night vision may be reduced both by fatigue and oxygen deficiency, also by sunbathing or other exposure to bright light; sensible use of sunglasses or avoidance of such exposure is the solution.

Passive smoking

Recent medical opinion has suggested that involuntary breathing by non-smokers of other people's tobacco smoke, termed passive smoking, is detrimental to their health. A smoker produces two types of smoke. The term 'mainstream' is applied to smoke which is caused by the inhalation of a cigarette; the smoke produced passes into the smoker's respiratory system and is then exhaled. 'Sidestream' smoke is the smoke which comes off the end of a cigarette between puffs. As the smoker filters most of the mainstream smoke with his lungs and retains the majority of the toxic substances, it is then the sidestream smoke which contains most of the detrimental matter as far as the non-smoker is concerned.

As more research is made into passive smoking and the effects become more known it is possible that airlines will emulate industry by introducing some form of positive control of smoking in the flight deck and passenger cabin.

In the meantime, the advice would be to avoid, where practicable, working with people who habitually smoke. A request by a pilot to his colleague on the flight deck to extinguish his cigarette or pipe would therefore be a matter of tact, politeness and strength of character.

7 Tropical Medicine

Although, by definition, 'tropical' diseases occur mainly in tropical areas, they are not necessarily confined to these zones. Some exotic diseases can be contracted in temperate climates. However, with the continual travelling involved in airline flying we stand a greater chance of meeting these diseases, hence the need for stricter precautions.

Tropical diseases may be transmitted by insects such as flies and mosquitoes, by contact with people or animals suffering from disease, or by infected food or water. Stomach and intestinal infections are almost invariably contracted through the mouth from infected material. Some diseases can be prevented by inoculations or by the use of prophylactic drugs. The gastro-intestinal infections can be avoided by careful eating habits and a high standard of personal hygiene. It is better not to patronise those establishments where food care standards are low and sanitation is poor (such places are often found quite close to the hotel, and can, regrettably, sometimes be found in the hotel itself).

Should you be unfortunate enough to fall ill shortly after visiting a tropical or sub-tropical area (particularly if malarial), remember to *emphasise* this fact to the doctor treating you. He may well be unaccustomed to treating tropical diseases, and this information will aid his diagnosis.

The following is a list of the more common diseases and illnesses which can be contracted in tropical regions, with a short description of their nature, symptoms and how best to avoid them.

Malaria

This kills more people throughout the world than any other known disease. Furthermore, it is on the increase, in spite of the fact that available prophylactics can provide ready amelioration. In particular, several large areas that were almost free of malaria a few years ago have now been re-infected. The areas where the disease is endemic are widespread throughout tropical and sub-tropical regions.

Malaria is a highly unpleasant, feverish infection caused by a parasite in the blood stream. The parasite is transmitted through a mosquito bite from an insect that has previously bitten a malarial victim. Acute symptoms develop after a period of six to eleven days when the parasite invades the red blood cells. Following repeated attacks anaemia develops, the liver and spleen become enlarged, and there is general ill-health. Adults living in the tropics develop a limited immunity but Europeans travelling are particularly at risk. There are several types of malaria; the most severe kind carrying a considerable risk of mortality. The others tend to cause non-fatal but recurring attacks. It is worth remembering that even though you may survive an attack of malaria, *the disease could be with you for the rest of your life.*

Avoidance of mosquito bites is less of a problem whilst staying in air-conditioned hotels, but one can still be bitten at any time in other environments and during airport transits. Insecticidal sprays should be used in rooms that are not air-conditioned and the skin should be protected from mosquito bites by the use of nets, suitable clothing and insect repellent. When visiting or passing through malarious areas it is *imperative* that the currently prescribed, anti-malarial drugs are *regularly* taken, as instructed. These drugs are effective and have no unpleasant side effects. It is not worth the risk to neglect these simple precautions. **ARE YOU TAKING YOUR ANTI-MALARIAL TABLETS?**

Food poisoning

In warm climates there is a greatly increased risk of bacterial contamination from the unclean fingers of food handlers with low standards of personal and kitchen hygiene. There is also the possibility of worm infection in meat (e.g. tapeworm in pork). Bacteria thrive in conditions of moisture and warmth, but lie dormant in refrigerated or frozen food. When this food is warmed the dormant bacteria start to multiply, hence the danger of re-heated food. Furthermore, some of the toxins found in food are very resistant to heat.

Most of us have, from time to time, suffered from the milder forms of gastro-enteritis. On occasions it can be most severe, with sudden onset of nausea, vomiting, diarrhoea and pain in the abdomen. Some poisons complete the incapacitation by attacking the central nervous system and causing disturbed vision and impaired sense of balance. According to the type of poisoning the symptoms may develop almost immediately, or be delayed several hours.

When on service, do not eat the same food as your colleagues, either on the aircraft or during the twelve hours prior to duty. Try to patronise only those restaurants where you know the standard of hygiene is high and the food is fresh. Elsewhere avoid the following:

(a) All uncooked or undercooked food, such as salads, raw vegetables, raw meat, raw fish etc.

(b) Cut fruit, and fruit that is thin-skinned, bruised or over-ripe. Skinned fruits that can be washed and peeled should be safe.

(c) Most fish dishes, particularly shellfish. These can harbour powerful poisons without impairing the taste.

(d) Mayonnaise, cream sauces and ice-cream.

If, in spite of all precautions, you find yourself suffering from diarrhoea and vomiting, **DO NOT FLY.** Consult a doctor. Drink plenty of boiled water to make good fluid losses – if you can add a little salt to it, so much the better. The commercially available drugs may help, but do not rely on them, or take too many. Finally, inform your company medical branch and your pilot association with details of the meal, location, time etc. so that any necessary action can be taken to prevent a recurrence.

Cholera

This is an acute epidemic disease caused by a bacterium spread by the faeces of infected people. The first symptom is the sudden onset of copious, watery diarrhoea. There may be no pain or nausea to start with, but vomiting and muscle cramps will follow later. Immediate medical attention is imperative since the resultant dehydration can prove fatal. Immunization against cholera is only moderately effective, hence the need to exercise great care in infected areas. The partial protection of inoculation should however be secured with a booster every six months. In regions where cholera occurs use only purified or boiled water. Avoid uncooked fruit and vegetables and food that may be contaminated by fingers or flies. Maintain a high standard of personal hygiene.

Typhoid

This is a serious infectious disease caused by a type of salmonella bacterium. The source of the disease is the urine and faeces of typhoid sufferers and 'carriers'; transmission is through contaminated water, milk and other foods. The predominant symptom is a fever, which gradually rises day by day for a week or so, then continues for a further period with only small morning remissions. Transient rose spots may be seen on the skin. Often early stages may be accompanied by severe headaches, coughing and nose bleeding. As the fever persists the patient becomes very listless and eventually delirious – the so-called 'typhoid state'. Without early diagnosis and treatment serious complications may occur, including internal haemorrhage and perforation of the bowel, both of which carry a high fatality rate. Inoculation is effective to a considerable degree, and may modify the course of the disease if it is contracted. Typhoid occurs throughout the tropical and sub-tropical world, and those exposed should have a yearly booster inoculation. The monovalent typhoid vaccine is probably better than the more usual TAB vaccine.

Paratyphoid

The cause and symptoms of paratyphoid are similar to those of typhoid, but the effects are usually less severe. Some protection may be given by TAB vaccine (a combination of the antigens of typhoid and paratyphoid A and B), but how much is uncertain. What is important is that a suspected attack be diagnosed early.

Infective hepatitis

This is a viral infection of the liver, common throughout the tropics and under-developed world. It may be contracted through the intake of polluted water or food, or by droplet infection from coughing and sneezing. The best method of prevention is a high standard of personal hygiene.

Initial symptoms are often vague. There will usually be fever, with diarrhoea and occasional vomiting. The patient feels 'rough' and there is marked loss of appetite. When the disease is established the patient turns yellow (jaundice) with some tenderness over the liver, reddish-brown urine and rather pale stools. *Do not delay seeking medical attention*, for hepatitis is a debilitating disease and can have serious consequences for the liver. It is an unpleasant illness requiring a long convalescence and complete abstinence from alcohol for a period of six months or more.

Poliomyelitis

This is an acute infection of the central nervous system sometimes resulting in paralysis. It is caused by a virus that enters through the nose or mouth and attacks the muscle-controlling nerves. The disease sometimes occurs in epidemics, but more often in sporadic form. The European traveller is at high risk. Immunization is effective and given via the mouth. It should be repeated every five years. The immunization is simple and painless, so there is no excuse for not taking this elementary precaution. **IS YOUR POLIO VACCINATION UP TO DATE?**

Tetanus

Although common in tropical countries, tetanus can be found everywhere. It is caused by a type of bacterium in the soil and enters the body through wounds, especially puncture wounds, that are contaminated by soil. The infection causes spasms of the voluntary muscles and results in convulsions. There is a high risk of death. Immunization gives a very high degree of protection. Wounds which are contaminated with dirt, rust or splinters should be treated by a doctor and even though you have been previously inoculated against tetanus, you should still have a booster injection of *tetanus toxoid*. If you have been adequately immunized against tetanus you do not need, and should not accept, tetanus anti-toxin (ATS). Tetanus vaccination should be boosted every five years.

Smallpox

This highly contagious and very unpleasant virus disease is characterised by a rash that leaves pitted scars on the skin, and sometimes results in blindness. It is spread by contact with an infected person or with articles he or she has touched, and also by inhaling germs. The vaccination is effective, with re-vaccination required every three years. At present the disease is well confined and international vaccination regulations may eventually be changed.

Yellow fever

This is a virus disease, carried by mosquitoes, and found mainly in South America and Africa. In serious cases the virus exerts its effects on the liver and kidneys causing intense jaundice with yellow skin and eyes. The vaccination is completely effective and should be renewed every ten years.

Rabies

This disease is caused by a bite from an infected animal. It has widespread geographical distribution and is a **KILLER**. Its carriers are not only domestic cats and dogs, but also various small wild animals that make urban areas their home. Following a long incubation period, the onset of the disease is marked by headache, loss of appetite, a dry throat and thirst. This is followed by the classical spasmodic attacks of convulsions, aversion to water, and mental lucidity. Death occurs primarily as a result of respiratory failure due to muscular spasms.

The time until onset of the symptoms depends upon the site of the bite, and varies from nine days for a cut in the neck or head, to *more than a year* if the wound is in the foot. The journey of the rabies virus from the wound to the brain may be stopped by prompt vaccination; delay in treatment can be fatal for the patient and serious for the whole community. Until recently rabies treatment was most unpleasant, but modern vaccines are less painful and have fewer side effects. Four intramuscular injections are given over a period of two weeks, with boosters after one month and three months.

Remember, just the saliva from a rabid animal on broken skin can cause infection, so **WHEN IN INFECTED AREAS AVOID ALL UNNECESSARY ANIMAL CONTACT.**

Bilharziasis (Schistosomiasis)

This group of diseases is spread by parasite worms living in sewage-contaminated water that contains the appropriate snails in which the parasites multiply. It is widespread in South America, Africa and Asia. It can be extremely unpleasant, affecting the liver, the bladder and the intestines. The larva of the worm enters the body by penetrating the skin of anyone entering the contaminated water. So swim in a swimming pool with a proper purification system; **DO NOT SWIM IN RIVERS, LAKES OR HARBOURS.**

Hookworm, mycetoma and other allied diseases are caused by walking barefoot on contaminated ground. It is advisable to wear something on your feet both in and out of doors. Exercise particular care when walking on tropical beaches and over coral.

Dehydration

Excessive perspiration in hot climates leads to loss of fluid and salt by the body, resulting in a loss of energy and a feeling of fatigue. It can also give rise to heat exhaustion, lassitude, giddiness and cramps. Aim to drink about six pints of fluid every day (remembering that dehydration is aggravated by alcohol) and ensure that adequate salt is eaten at meals. If this is done salt tablets are usually unnecessary, and in any event *do not take salt tablets without also increasing your fluid intake.*

Sunburn

Although well known to everyone, sunburn still claims a regular quota of victims. Apart from the normal precautions, bear in mind that at *hot and high* places (Central Africa, Andes, etc) the sun is particularly strong and can cause severe sunburn in temperatures that may feel quite temperate.

Heat stroke

This is a serious condition caused by extreme elevation of body temperature due to failure of the body's heat-regulating mechanism. Under normal circumstances it is unlikely to happen; however, there are predisposing factors such as obesity, lack of acclimatization, alcohol intake and lack of sleep. If such factors are associated with, for example, strenuous exercise in the heat of the day, then collapse with heat stroke becomes a distinct possibility. Should this happen, remove the victim to the shade at once, and keep his skin wet and well-fanned. *Obtain immediate medical attention.* Avoidance of heat stroke is mostly a matter of moderation and common sense.

Prickly heat

This is a skin condition caused by poor ventilation of the skin when perspiring. It can best be avoided by washing with bland soap, drying well and using dusting powder or calamine. Change underclothing frequently, and avoid wearing garments made of nylon.

8 First Aid in Airline Practice

General

The airline pilot has need of some working knowledge of first aid, primarily in order to decide whether a sick passenger or crew member in flight would benefit significantly from an early landing. In addition, this knowledge is useful in the wider context of everyday life.

There are, or could be, legal repercussions, if the pilot, inexpert as he most probably is in medical matters, attempts to offer more than very basic first aid, which any untrained person might be expected to give. At times, help may be forthcoming from medically-trained cabin crew members.

Therefore, if your immediate impression indicates that the sick person is seriously ill, FIRST OF ALL check whether there is a doctor or other medically-trained person on board and enlist his or her help. If this help is not available, a safe, early landing where adequate medical facilities exist should be your next consideration. There will be occasions when neither of the above alternatives is available, and you have to do the best you can in the circumstances. Before attempting diagnosis and treatment, as outlined in the following paragraphs, you should try to protect your legal position by extracting some form of consent, whether express or implied, from the would-be patient.

Legal implications

Although it would be unthinkable to deliberately withhold assistance from a person in need, you should be aware of the legal position which is, in one word, confusing.

Anglo-American common law, that is to say, the common law systems that have developed from British law and are practised in most British Commonwealth countries and the United States, not only denies any obligation to give aid to a stranger, it may even hold the administrator of first aid (or the aircraft Commander) responsible if death or injury results from such efforts. In most European countries, on the other hand, it is a criminal offence *not* to render assistance to those in need. So, if first aid is given, the legal position will depend, at least in theory, on geographical location. In practice, legal problems are unlikely to occur provided the following points are borne in mind:

(a) In his efforts to alleviate the suffering of a passenger, the aircraft Commander must *not* put other people, or his aircraft, at risk.

(b) If a medical emergency occurs, the first step should be to try and locate expert medical guidance (preferably from amongst the passengers, failing that by radio).

(c) Aircraft carry some potent and dangerous drugs, which, in unskilled hands, may do more harm than good, so, if expert advice is *not* available, medically-unqualified personnel would do well to approach their first aid with caution. Common-sense and legal prudence both suggest that you restrict your effort to that which any untrained person might be expected to give. Remember: in law, 'inexperience is accounted a fault'.

In-flight illness

Evaluation of any illness or injury in flight should start with talking to the sick person. Your introduction and questioning should be of a concerned and reassuring nature. Do not show anxiety in your manner or voice.

Try to obtain a simple history, in particular:

(a) Has he had this before?

(b) Has he seen a doctor about it?

(c) What did the doctor say?

(d) Is medicine being prescribed?

If this confirms a mild to moderate attack of a recurrent illness, encourage the patient to take his medication. This, together with your concern and reassurance will usually suffice until your destination is reached.

If the illness is new or strange to the person, or you are uncertain about the degree of seriousness and there is no doctor on board, use the information below to evaluate the severity of the case in relation to the remaining flight time, in deciding whether or not to divert to the nearest alternate.

PAIN

Pain is common and is nature's danger signal indicating malfunction of or injury to the various body organs. It causes fear and apprehension in people. Usually there are four easily visible manifestations of severe pain:

(a) A look of impending disaster, i.e. he looks as though he thinks he is going to die.

(b) Skin colour is usually pale, especially the face, with diffuse perspiration.

(c) Breathing is usually a bit faster and deeper.

(d) He may be writhing about or crying.

A person experiencing severe or excruciating pain should receive early medical attention. Mild to moderate pain will need to be dealt with according to the history of the patient.

Powerful drugs may be carried in your aircraft medical kit, accompanied by printed instructions in their use. **Exercise caution in the use of these pain killers,** and when it is evident they are necessary, ensure the instructions for their application are strictly followed.

Morphia, should *not* be administered under the following circumstances:

(a) Head injuries and unconscious patients.

(b) Persons under sixteen years of age.

(c) Severe abdominal pain due to disease (e.g.appendicitis).

(d) Severe respiratory distress (chest injuries).

(e) Advanced cases of pregnancy.

(f) Within six hours of a previous morphine injection.

HEART TROUBLE

Chest pain due to heart disease is a moderate to severe cramping pain in the centre or left of the chest, which may also radiate or 'shoot' into the left shoulder, arm, forearm or fingers. Less often it radiates down both arms or up into the neck. People with angina pectoris usually carry special tablets or capsules which give prompt relief.

Treat a heart attack as follows:

(a) Give oxygen immediately.

(b) Place in a relaxed semi-reclining position with upper body raised.

(c) Loosen clothing at waist and neck.

(d) Obtain prompt medical attention.

RESPIRATORY DIFFICULTIES

If a person has stopped breathing, prompt action is essential to save life (see overleaf for Emergency Resuscitation).

If a passenger is short of breath enough to complain about it, then he is likely to have a severe illness.

Severe respiratory difficulty is indicated by:

(a) Rapid breathing.

(b) Poor skin colour (ashen, grey or blue-grey).

EMERGENCY RESUSCITATION

1. Lay patient on back on firm surface.

2. Open airway, by:
(a) Clear mouth of matter and mucus.
(b) Lift neck with one hand.
(c) Further extend head back by pushing forehead down with other hand.

3. Apply 'Kiss of Life':
(a) Close off nostrils with fingers.
(b) Take deep breaths and cover patient's mouth with your mouth.
(c) Exhale into patient's mouth and observe chest expand and fall again.
(d) Repeat every five seconds.

4. After five breaths are given check for heartbeat by:
(a) Feeling for pulse either side of the Adam's apple.
(b) Raise upper eyelid and observe constriction (narrowing) of pupil of the eye.

5. If pulse is absent and pupils remain dilated (wider), begin external heart compression:
(a) Place heel of hand over lower half of patient's breast-bone.
(b) Rock forwards and press downwards on the lower part of the breast-bone. In an adult the breast-bone may be pressed towards the spine for up to one and a half inches. Release.
(c) Repeat every second.

6. If patient requires both mouth-to-mouth and external cardiac compression:
(a) One rescuer should alternate between inflating lungs twice and compressing heart fifteen times.
(b) Two rescuers should inflate lungs on the release of every fifth external cardiac compression.

7. Remember – breathing for a person who has no heartbeat or compressing the heart of someone who is not breathing, does no good. Both must be done if indicated.

(c) He will forcefully tell you he needs more air or wants oxygen.

Give oxygen immediately. If he remains conscious, and feels and looks better, then it is usually safe to continue to destination. However, should his condition deteriorate, prompt medical attention is required.

HYPERVENTILATION

Hyperventilation (emotional over-breathing), usually caused by fear or anxiety, might be confused with lack of oxygen. However, hyperventilators usually have normal skin colour and experience numbness and tingling in the face and/or hands and feet. These are not symptomatic of true oxygen deficiency. Reassurance, slowing down the breathing, and breathing in and out of a paper bag or empty oxygen mask will effect a quick recovery (by increasing the carbon dioxide content in the blood to normal levels). If there is no rapid recovery, assume oxygen lack and give oxygen.

UNCONSCIOUSNESS

This is an easy diagnosis, but it is usually very difficult to ascertain the cause. Generally, an unconscious passenger is a poor risk, and requires prompt medical attention. If there is the smell of alcohol on his breath, do not automatically assume that he is just drunk. Suggested action is:

(a) Do not leave patient unattended. Frequently check pulse and breathing.

(b) Do not give anything by mouth. Give no drugs.

(c) Give oxygen.

(d) If there is any difficulty in breathing, lay patient in three quarters prone position, as shown:

$\frac{3}{4}$ prone position - do **not** use a pillow

(e) Look for a special bracelet, dog-tag round the neck or card in his wallet which may give special medical information.

(f) Loosen tight clothing and cover with a blanket.

CONVULSIONS (FITS, EPILEPTIC SEIZURE)
These can vary from slight twitching of the face and arms to massive, violent jerks of all the muscles of the body, with grotesque facial expressions and eyes opening and closing. The person is often ashen grey due to inadequate respiratory movements and may urinate and have an involuntary bowel movement.
   Treatment:

(a) Restrain gently.

(b) If it is a violent convulsion, leave him in his seat. If he is unconscious and breathing inefficiently, attempt to gently hold the head erect if possible.

(c) Do not place any object in his mouth. He will not swallow his tongue.

(d) The convulsion will usually stop gradually in ten to fifteen minutes. Normal respiration should begin within a minute, and the person may wake up, appear confused, and then drop off to sleep. If breathing is normal, let him sleep, as he will be extremely tired. Observe him frequently to check that there is adequate respiration.

(e) If breathing is not normal and the windpipe is blocked with mucus, clear this with the finger. If unsuccessful, lie the person prone with head downwards and strike three or four sharp blows between the shoulders. After removing any debris from the throat, if necessary apply mouth-to-mouth resuscitation.

If a convulsion lasts over fifteen to twenty minutes, then the person requires prompt medical attention.

INSULIN SHOCK OF DIABETES
This is caused by the blood sugar dropping to an abnormally low level. The person may be nervous, shaky, irritable, irrational or give the appearance of having had too much to drink. He should immediately be given several packets of sugar in a glass of water, since he may soon become unconscious, and cannot then be given anything by mouth. Sugar water will relieve the condition in about five minutes. If the person becomes unconscious (this may be accompanied by a convulsion) he requires prompt medical attention. Do not try to tell the

difference between insulin shock (too little sugar) and diabetic coma (too much sugar). It is far more likely to be insulin shock, and needs sugar immediately. If it is the rare case that is not, he is already 'floating in sugar' and the extra glass of sugar water will not make much difference. However, he does need prompt medical attention.

EXTERNAL BLEEDING
The aim is to stop blood flowing. This is done by pressure and elevation to aid clot formation and by rest, since movement breaks up the clot.

(a) Press the area where the blood comes from. Use a sterile dressing. If from an arm or leg, lift up the limb (unless broken). See diagram.

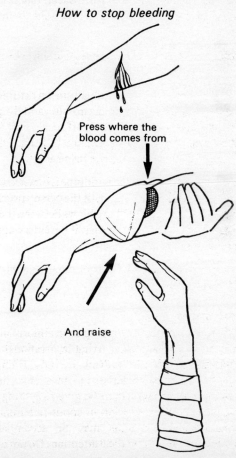

How to stop bleeding

Press where the blood comes from

And raise

(b) Rest the injured person so that the blood clot which has formed will not be disturbed.

(c) If the wound continues to bleed through the dressing, apply another dressing and more pressure. *Do not* remove existing dressing.

(d) Reassure the person and tell him to lie quietly. The importance of gentle and careful handling of the person injured cannot be overstressed. Rough handling increases pain and apprehension.

(e) If a wound contains any foreign bodies, remove them only if they are loose and easy to lift out. Dressings must be built up around any foreign bodies or broken bone ends using a ring pad so that when the bandage is applied pressure is applied all round the wound, but not on the foreign body or broken bone end. Use a crepe bandage. Apply a sling if applicable. See diagrams for details of slings and dressings.

(f) Dressings used to stop bleeding should be checked at intervals to ensure that the bleeding has ceased.

Collar and cuff

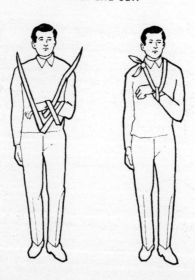

66

Triangular sling (St John sling)

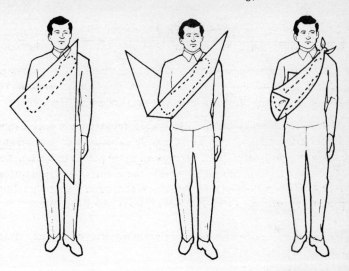

Head bandage

Arm bandage

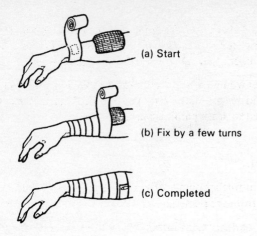

(a) Start

(b) Fix by a few turns

(c) Completed

Foot bandage

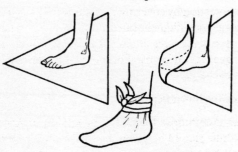

NOSE BLEED

The person should grasp the nose firmly just below the hard part, at the same time keeping the head forward over a basin or bowl. This should be kept up for ten minutes. Release slowly. Repeat for another five minutes, if necessary. Advise the patient not to breathe through the nose, and to resist any temptation to sniff, or blow the nose.

INTERNAL BLEEDING

There are two types: that which occurs around the ends of broken bones and bleeding into body cavities (such as chest or lungs).

The bleeding can be visible or concealed:

68

(a) Visible by the person vomiting or coughing blood, or the presence of bruising.

(b) Concealed internal bleeding – the person looks ill and pale, the skin is cold, the pulse is rapid and feeble. No first aid treatment is possible for internal bleeding; the person needs hospital treatment.

A pregnant woman who is bleeding should always be treated seriously. She should be promptly removed for medical treatment, since she could bleed to death painlessly and quickly.

BURNS
Treatment:

(a) Prevent further damage by removing the person from the cause or the cause from the person.

(b) Heat and friction burns should be treated immediately by immersion in water which is cooler than body temperature. Chemical burns should have the chemical washed off at once.

(c) Prevent infection by covering the burn with a sterile dressing large enough to cover more than the burnt area. Cover one small area at a time rather than the whole area at once. Burn dressings should always be padded or have several layers of dressing materials applied in order to absorb any discharge.

(d) Reassure the burnt person.

(e) In order to minimise the effects of fluid loss from burnt tissues, conscious adults should be given drinks of water, weak tea or milk in quantities of about half a cupful every ten minutes.

(f) If there is a large area burn on a limb, immobilise the limb as if it were fractured.

Important DON'TS in treatment for burns

Do not burst blisters.

Do not apply any lotion or antiseptic.

Do not touch the burnt area.

Do not undress or handle the person more than necessary.

Do not apply cotton wool or fluffy material.

Do not cough or breathe over the burnt area.

FRACTURES

A fracture is a broken or cracked bone. A closed fracture has no wound at or near it, whereas an open fracture is a fracture plus wound. A fracture may be present if any part of the body has had a heavy blow or thump and the part is:

(a) Painful.

(b) Tender to touch.

(c) Misshapen or swollen.

(d) The person cannot use the part normally.

If in doubt, always treat as if the bone were broken.

The aim of first aid for fractures is to cover all open fractures and keep the fractured parts still. Therefore, treat the wound initially to stop bleeding and prevent infection, then treat both types of fractures in the same way; that is to prevent movement from occurring at or near the ends of the broken bone. It is usually necessary to prevent any movement for some distance above and below the break. Never tie over the break.

(a) Fractures of upper limb

Put the arm in a sling, see diagram. If the break is near the elbow, do not try to bend the elbow in order to apply a sling. Tell the person to lie down and place the arm gently on a pillow. Another method is to put some padding between the arm and the side of the body and gently move the injured arm into the side on to the padding. Then tie the arm loosely to the trunk.

(b) Fractures of lower limb. The best method to stop movement is to tie the good leg to the injured one. See diagram.

70

Arm sling

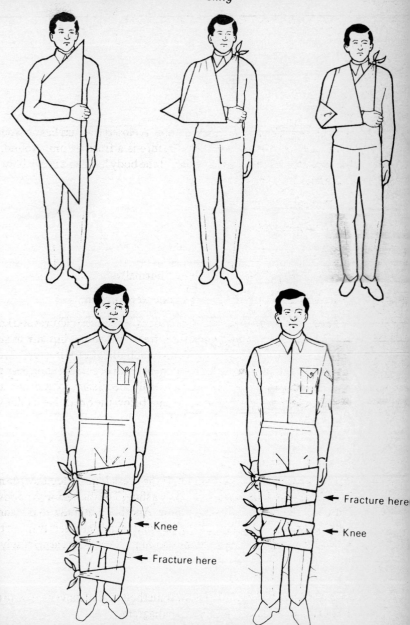

Knee

Fracture here

Fracture here

Knee

71

(c) Ankle and Leg. If the break is near the ankle, place one or two pillows under the leg. Tie these loosely on to the leg to stop the leg rolling off or moving. Tie the feet and ankle with a figure of eight bandage. See diagram.

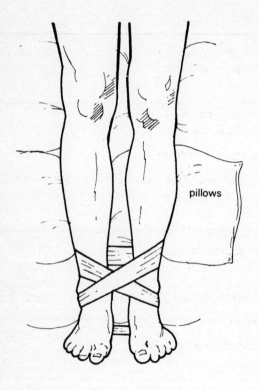

pillows

(d) Thigh, Hip and Pelvis. The person has to be kept still from the armpits to the feet in order to stop movement. Tie the feet and legs together lying down.

POISONING

(a) Corrosive poisoning (by acid or alkali).
This is characterised by severe burning pain in mouth, throat, chest and abdomen, with retching and vomiting Burns on the lips and mouth may also be visible.

Do not give an emetic. Give quantities of water or milk to dilute the chemical. If the poison is identified, give a suitable antidote (alkaline poison – give acid: vinegar, lemon; acid poison – give alkali; bicarbonate of soda, magnesia tablets) and treat for shock.

(b) Non-corrosive poisons (e.g. drugs overdose).
Give an emetic (two tablespoons of salt dissolved in glass of water).

Give black coffee to keep patient awake, give oxygen and treat for shock. Check pulse and breathing.

AIRSICKNESS

This is probably the most common illness in flight. Signs and symptoms occur in the following order:

(a) Passenger does not feel well.

(b) He feels mild to severe nausea.

(c) He feels hot, but his skin is cool and moist.

(d) Vomiting, usually without true pain in the stomach.

(e) He often feels better after vomiting.

Treatment:

(a) Loosen tight clothing.

(b) Recline seat.

(c) Apply cool cloth to forehead.

(d) Reassure.

(e) If a long flight remains, give an airsickness pill with a sip of water and hope it stays down. Do not repeat.

(f) Consider repositioning passenger to a better location where the amount of aircraft movement is reduced.

SHOCK

This is a state of collapse, resulting in a reduction in blood pressure, caused by pain, emotional experience, haemorrhage, etc. It can range from nervous shock starting at the moment of injury (e.g. fainting) to established (or surgical) shock, a very dangerous condition following injury, which may take several hours to manifest itself.

Signs and symptoms are:

(a) Skin – pale, cold, clammy, sweating and becoming an ashen grey colour.

(b) Pulse – rapid and weak (100–120 to the minute).

(c) Breathing – rapid and shallow.

(d) Shivering, dizziness, nausea, vomiting.

(e) Dull, quiet, apathetic attitude.

(f) Progressing to unconsciousness.

Treatment:

(a) Increase local blood pressure by lowering head between knees for nervous shock; and place patient in a comfortable position lying down with lower limbs raised (except in cases of chest and head injuries) for established shock.

(b) Keep warm (do not overheat).

(c) Loosen tight clothing and give air (oxygen unnecessary).

(d) Give sips of water or tea (no alcohol) except for abdominal cases.

(e) Reassure and relieve pain as much as possible.

(f) If no improvement, condition requires prompt medical attention.

ABNORMAL BEHAVIOUR

Many types of illness can affect a person's behaviour and personality. Someone attracting attention in the cabin by his behaviour should be observed and carefully evaluated to see if he shows signs of illness other than mental. Many people who act strangely in the aircraft are basically unstable personalities who function normally on the ground, but deteriorate under the 'fear of flight'. Question an abnormal person gently, and try to persuade him to talk. If he is quietly 'nuts', you should be safe in continuing the flight, but if he causes a continued and violent commotion, with nothing pacifying or quietening him, you should consider an early landing, with the authorities meeting the aircraft. The Tokyo Convention gives the Commander of an aircraft in flight internationally-recognised wide powers of arrest and restraint over persons who may jeopardise good order and discipline on board the aircraft.

Finally, bear in mind that a person behaving abnormally could be an intended hijacker, or an intended suicide carrying explosives in his luggage.

9 Some Aspects Of Aviation Psychology

Psychology is the study of behaviour. In the context of aviation, this behaviour may consist of visuo-motor tracking during an ILS approach, interacting with other individuals on the flight deck, or integrating the various sources of information in the cockpit. In short, everything that the pilot thinks or does is legitimate material for the study of the aviation psychologist.

Perception

The word perception is used to mean all of those processes that result in the creation of a mental model of the world. This model is clearly based very heavily on incoming sensory data (in the case of most of us, and especially the pilot, these are largely visual data), but is also shaped by our store of experience of the world (memory). Normally our model is reasonably accurate, but sometimes it may differ from the real world, and such a mis-match is termed an 'illusion'.

The 'vestibular' illusions are produced by the effect of the unusual dynamic environment of flight on the inner ear, and take two common forms. In the first, the pilot is IMC and allows the aircraft to roll at a low rate that he cannot detect. Because the roll goes undetected, the pilot perceives that he still has a wings-level attitude, and cannot believe the AI or ADI when he re-attends to it. In the second, the pilot is also IMC; he increases the thrust (probably because he initiates a missed approach) and thus rotates the resultant of the gravitational and inertial force-vectors that act on him. The pilot may perceive the new rotated, force-vector resultant to be the normal gravity vector, and experience an illusion of pitch-up. If he then eases forward on the control column to counter this feeling, disastrous consequences may follow.

'Visual' illusions are also important for pilots. They can take many forms, but are especially associated with the judgement of range or depth. One of the most important visual 'cues' to range is that objects grow smaller (on the retina) as they become more distant: assumed actual size may be compared with retinal size to produce a perception of depth. If an incorrect assumption is made about the actual size of the object, then incorrect range estimates will inevitably follow. The commonest manifestation of this effect occurs just before touchdown on a runway that is very wide, when the feeling of increased proximity this produces can lead to a high flare. It can also be produced over unfamiliar terrain (for example when the size of scrub is overestimated, producing a perception of greater than actual height), or over any other textured surface, such as desert or sea, if the assumed size of the textural elements is wrong.

A mis-match between expectations and circumstances may cause other illusions for the pilot. For example, the cues – from runway and terrain – that he has learned to use in judging approach angle may well depend on the assumption that the terrain or runway is flat. Thus, sloping runways or terrain may produce steep or shallow approaches. Short landings, however, generally require the presence of other factors. Typically, the pilot will have made a shallow approach, but he will also have been concerned to touch down near the threshold (perhaps because of a critical runway length or poor braking conditions). In addition, he will have failed to perceive his proximity to the ground late in the approach because of unusual runway width or poor ground texture, perhaps because of snow cover or an over-water approach.

The illusions so far discussed arise because of the misinterpretation of a particular stimulus, but sometimes it is clear that the whole model of the world created by the pilot is in error. There are several cases, for example, of crews (one in a 747) who have attempted to take off while lined up on the runway edge lighting. An instance also exists of a crew who, in poor visibility, mistook four white vans parked on the peri track for a set of white PAPIs; mistaking one airport for another is a prevalent form of this error. The commonest form of accident – controlled flight into the ground – usually occurs to pilots who possess inappropriate mental models of their position in space. It is also interesting to note that most pilots who have flown into the ground in recent times, have done so while the GPWS was sounding! It seems generally to be true that once we have generated a model of the world which we believe to be adequate, contradictory information will be misinterpreted or ignored. We are interested only in information that substantiates our ideas about the world – an effect known as 'confirmation bias'.

If you begin to receive information that does not confirm or fit your model of the world, do not assume that the information is wrong. Try instead (perhaps by backtracking to a position of which you are certain) to ensure that your internal model is accurate. It is most difficult to do this when mental resources, and hence spare capacity, are at their lowest because of fatigue or preoccupation. The problem of fatigue and sleep management is dealt with elsewhere, but it should be noted that tiredness makes pilots less critical of their own behaviour, more likely to rely on habit and experience, and less likely to evaluate critically the information with which they are provided.

Skill

Flying is a skilled task, both in the sense that competence requires aptitude and experience, and in the more technical sense that the pilot develops 'motor programmes' that control sequences of actions. Such programmes are generally activated by a deliberate decision, but are then able to proceed automatically, requiring only occasional conscious monitoring. The resulting liberation of mental resources enables the pilot to think about one thing while he actually does another. It is fortunate that we are able to organise our activities in this way, but there are a number of problems associated with such automaticity. For example, the pilot who decides to transfer fuel but instead finds that he has shut a LP cock, has made the correct decision, but engaged the wrong programme. Similarly, if we engage the correct programme, but become preoccupied and fail to monitor its progress, we may find that the programme has taken the habitual, rather than the intended, path – the pilot may intend to make a flapless landing, but finds that he inadvertently lowers the flaps as normal. A programme may also be executed so frequently in a particular situation that simply being in the appropriate environment is enough to trigger it. It is notable in this context that calling 'three Greens' becomes so habitual on finals that almost all pilots who have landed gearless have called 'three greens' before doing so.

A further problem with automatic behaviour is that the pilot remembers his intention rather than his action. Apart from making accident investigation difficult, this may prevent the pilot whose aircraft begins to behave unusually from realising that the cause of the problem was his own recent behaviour.

Like some of the problems already described, motor programme

78

errors are most likely when the pilot is tired (and therefore has less mental capacity available for monitoring his own behaviour), or when his conscious attention is occupied with some subsidiary aspect of the flying task or even some non-flying matter such as a domestic problem. Finally, it should be noted that because these programme problems require behaviour to be automated, they can happen only to those with experience; the more experience you have, the more likely you are to become a victim.

Improve your chances by not dwelling on personal problems in the air, by training yourself to monitor your own actions, and by injecting a check into routine, but critical, patterns of behaviour (grasp gear lever – conscious check – lower lever).

Personality

Psychologists consider the ways in which people differ mostly in terms of intelligence and personality. About three quarters of the population are not as smart as the average commercial pilot, and the pilot group tends to be relatively homogeneous in this respect since a certain minimum intelligence is required to gain a licence. Pilot personalities are fairly variable however. There is a good deal of agreement among personality theorists that the first main dimension of personality is extraversion (a combination of sociability and impulsiveness), and that the next main dimension concerns tension and anxiety. Less dominant factors are independence and toughness of outlook.

There are many demonstrated relationships between personality type and variables such as the likelihood of being involved in a road accident, the probability of having a heart attack, or the chance that you will one day experience emotional problems. Generally speaking, extreme personality types do not make the best pilots. Individuals who are very tense and easily ruffled are not likely to choose the occupation, but some pilots may find that the way of life can itself cause anxiety. If you feel, or your spouse informs you, that you are more tense than you should be, deliberate relaxation may well help and you should try the techniques that are described in many of the texts on the airport bookstall. Simple progressive muscle relaxation may be sufficient (lie down, relax your feet, then calves, thighs and so on until you reach your face, then, fully relaxed, concentrate on something you find pleasant to think about while you breathe regularly). The same technique can help you to get to sleep if this is causing problems.

Tense individuals who are also extraverted will appear aggressive and easily angered. They may be impelled into unwise actions by becoming obsessed with a trivial matter that has upset them but which would be best forgotten. Those who are very extraverted but also extremely stable may be hazardous for a rather different reason: they tend to be adventurous and seek excitement, and may not have sufficient anxiety to be aware of the riskiness of their behaviour – risk may even have an attraction for them. Anxious introverts will tend to appear rather sullen, preoccupied, and uncommunicative, and the stable introvert rather thoughtful, but controlled.

Personality is difficult, but not impossible, to change. We can, to some extent, choose how to portray ourselves, and may thus modify our personality simply by deciding to do so. This begs the question of what sort of personality the pilot should select. The 'right stuff' may have been appropriate when civil flying consisted of fighting a DC3 through thunderstorms, but is signally inappropriate to modern operations in which safety considerations are paramount. If you need excitement, take up sky-diving, but decide that a more sedate persona is appropriate for the flight deck.

Social factors

Social psychology is the psychology of groups, and two pilots make a group. The way in which pilots interact on the flight deck will depend on a number of factors, notably personality (discussed above), status (captain, first officer), and role (handling, non-handling). A number of accidents appear to demonstrate that a common social problem of the flight deck concerns the difficulty that a first officer may encounter in telling his captain that an error is being made. It is obvious that the worst situation in this regard will be when a dominant captain, who is handling the aircraft, is paired with a submissive first officer. The situation may be almost as difficult when a young, and perhaps unsure, captain is paired with an old, dominant, and possibly resentful first officer.

It is not possible to detail all of the combinations of these factors that may cause difficulty, but there are certain principles that both pilots on the flight deck should bear in mind. For the captain, there are two modes of leadership behaviour that will be appropriate for him, and the choice between these depends on circumstances. If a strategic decision is being made, and time is not pressing, then a democratic style is called for in which the views of the other members of the flight deck are canvassed, and in which the captain explains the reasoning behind his decisions – especially if they differ from the expressed views of the crew. When an emergency presents itself, a more autocratic style is called for in which instructions are issued in the confident expectation that they will be followed without question. A common failure of captaincy is to use the second leadership style in the first set of circumstances, since this will guarantee alienation of a crew that has been trained to think, and they may even lay traps for the captain in order to cut him down to size.

The problem for the first officer is to develop techniques that will enable him to express his views candidly to the captain without appearing to question his competence, or to challenge his authority. Most captains will welcome a tactful comment (even if they bluster to cover their error), and will regard it as the proper role of the first officer to express any operational worries that he has. But there may be a rare event when the first officer is certain that the captain is getting it wrong, but is equally certain that he will not welcome comment. The first officer will have to assess this situation carefully, but he should not forget those occasions on which other first officers believed that matters would probably resolve themselves satisfactorily and that upsetting the captain was not necessary, but who were proved wrong by the accident. Nagging is not required of the first officer, but timely comments most certainly are, and he must have sufficient self-assurance to give them.

This brief review of aviation psychology has done scant justice to the subject. It may, however, have indicated that it is a pursuit concerned with the practical problems of pilots. Many airlines are now conducting courses for their pilots that recognise the importance of aviation psychology in improving safety and job satisfaction, and this is a development to be welcomed. All that is asked of the individual pilot is an open mind and a readiness to contemplate the unlikely possibility that his own behaviour, skill, or relationships with colleagues may be open to improvement.

Appendix 1
Back-strengthening Exercises

As we said in chapter 1, exercise is very useful in alleviating back problems and maintaining good postural muscles and mobility of joints in the spine. The following exercises have been recommended by the Senior Physiotherapist of British Airways specially for that purpose. However, *do not continue with any exercise that causes you pain.*

(a) Standing upright, hands above your head, push your fingertips up towards the ceiling, breathing in as you stretch. Hold the stretched position, then slowly breathe out and relax.

(b) Adopt a sitting position, hands on knees and supporting the weight of your trunk. Pull stomach in hard while breathing out. Hold for four seconds, then relax slowly, breathing in. Repeat.

(c) Lie on your back on the floor, with knees bent and feet flat on the floor. Arch your back between shoulders and buttocks and *push* chest further up into the air. Hold for four seconds, then relax slowly. Pull stomach in hard, and flatten your back against the floor. Hold, then relax.

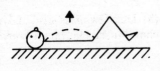

(d) Same position on the floor as the last exercise, lift head and right knee towards each other until they make contact, whilst pulling stomach in. Relax. Repeat with left knee. Do not do this exercise if you have back pain at the moment.

(e) Same position on the floor, with arms outstretched either side. Raise both knees, keep legs together and roll the lower half of your body to the left until the thigh rests on the floor. Then lift and roll to the right.

(f) Lie face down on the floor with arms by your side. Lift one leg up as far as you can in the air, keeping it straight. Hold for four seconds, then lower and relax. Repeat with the other leg. Then repeat with both legs together.

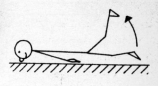

(g) Lie face down on the floor and lodge your feet securely under a heavy piece of furniture. Clasping your hands behind your back, brace shoulder blades together and tuck in chin. Now lift head and shoulders up off the floor as far as you can. Hold for four seconds, then relax slowly.

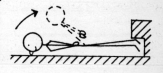

(h) Do a few press-ups, making sure the chin is tucked in and the body is straight.

(i) Now do some sideways press-ups. Lie on your side with the supporting arm straight, and legs straight together. Lift pelvis off the floor to straighten the body, up as high as you can and hold. Lower slowly, then repeat with weight on other arm.

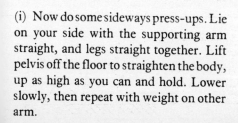

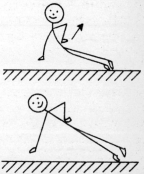

(j) Sit straddling a stool, with one arm bent at the elbow and the back of the hand tucked in under the armpit and with the other arm arched over the head. Start by sitting up straight, then bend sideways as far as you can, pushing with both hands, and keeping your seat down on the stool. Straighten up, change position of your arms, then bend the other way. Relax.

(k) Sit straddling the stool with arms out either side, and elbows bent with thumbs touching chest. Sit up straight, pull shoulder blades together, then twist to the left as far as you can. Hold, then twist round to the right as far as you can. Relax.

(l) In any convenient position perform bottom clenching exercises. Tighten your bottom by squeezing your buttocks together. Hold for four seconds, then relax.

Two final points on the avoidance of back troubles. When lifting heavy objects take great care to bend at the knees, keep the back upright and straight, and lift by straightening the knees to stand up. Your bed at home should be firm enough to support your body evenly along its length. If it sags uncomfortably in the middle, it is time to save some allowances and buy a new bed.

Appendix 2
AIDS

Acquired Immune Deficiency Syndrome or 'AIDS' is caused by the human immunodeficiency virus (HIV).

The syndrome can present in a number of ways: where the symptoms are non-specific, the risk factors associated with the individual patient may be taken into account in making a diagnosis. Intensive investigation with specialised equipment may often be required before a diagnosis can be confirmed.

The time taken to develop the syndrome can vary from weeks to many months. As far as is known at present, not all persons infected with HIV will develop the full syndrome, but the percentage of cases doing so could be fairly high. At the time of writing (1988) the disease is incurable and ends in death, usually due to a chronic infection, such as a form of pneumonia.

In the infected person, HIV is present in many body fluids but most commonly in the blood stream and semen. A blood test, which should be carried out only with the informed consent of the patient, can detect the antibodies produced in the blood by HIV.

By far the most common method of spreading AIDS is by homosexual intercourse, although heterosexual spread does occur. Drug addicts, who share needles, and use intravenous routes for their drug-taking are at equal risk with those who have direct sexual contact with an infected person.

AIDS occurs worldwide but is particularly prevalent in east and central Africa and on the west coast of the USA. There has been no evidence of spread of the virus by a third vector such as mosquitoes.

Infection is only spread by direct contact with infected body fluids. It is not spread through the air by sneezing or coughing, or on towels or clothing. Neither is there any danger in sharing washing facilities or handling goods.

In giving emergency first aid the standard precautions already needed to reduce the risk of transmitting other diseases, such as hepatitis, are effective against AIDS. Aircrew should give mouth-to-mouth resuscitation only through the mouthpieces provided in aircraft first aid kits.

Aircrew should be well versed in sensible hygiene precautions, especially when abroad. If these are observed then the risk of HIV infection is minimal.

In the U.K. the following organisations give advice and further information on AIDS:

Terrence Higgins Trust (BM/AIDS), Grays Inn Road, London WC1N 3XX.
This is a registered charity which offers help and counselling.

Legal Helpline 01 405 2381   Wednesday 7pm–10pm.

Helpline 01 242 1010   Seven days a week 3pm–10pm.

Healthline Telephone Service.   01 980 9848 2pm–10pm,
(Confidential 24-hour service.)   Freephone 0800 010976

      0345 581151   Charged at local
      0345 581876   call rate

Health Education Council, P.O. Box 100, Milton Keynes, MK2 2TX.
(for explanatory booklet)

Scottish AIDS Monitor, P.O. Box 169, Edinburgh, EH1 3UV.

Index